NEWSPAPER GENEALOGICAL COLUMN DIRECTORY

Sixth Edition

Revised and Updated

By Anita Cheek Milner, M.A., J.D.

HERITAGE BOOKS, INC.

Copyright 1985, 1987, 1989, 1992, 1996 by
Anita Cheek Milner

Sixth Edition

Published 1996 by

HERITAGE BOOKS, INC.
1540E Pointer Ridge Place
Bowie, Maryland 20716
1-800-398-7709

ISBN 0-7884-0507-1

A Complete Catalog Listing Hundreds of Titles
On History, Genealogy, and Americana
Available Free Upon Request

DEDICATION

FOR MY SONS-IN-LAW, STEVE GUNTON AND EDDIE PROFFITT, WITH LOVE AND GRATITUDE; FOR TAKING MY DAUGHTERS OFF MY HANDS, HAVING JOBS, AND FATHERING THE WORLD'S BEST GRANDSONS

TABLE OF CONTENTS

Introduction.. vii

Magazines... ix

Miscellaneous Columns

African-American Research...	1
Australian Research...	1
Canadian Research..	2
Computers...	2
Copyright..	3
Family Names..	3
General Research..	3
Heraldry..	4
Irish Research..	4
Jewish Research...	5
Native American...	5
Regional United States...	5
Scottish Research..	6

Columns Arranged by State

Alabama..	7
Arkansas...	10
California..	13
Connecticut...	15
District of Columbia...	16
Florida..	16
Georgia...	19
Hawaii..	25
Idaho..	25
Illinois..	26
Indiana..	29
Iowa...	39
Kansas..	42
Kentucky..	43
Louisiana..	47
Maine...	52

v

Maryland	54
Massachusetts	55
Michigan	56
Minnesota	57
Mississippi	57
Missouri	62
Montana	67
Nebraska	67
New Hampshire	69
New Jersey	69
New Mexico	69
New York	69
North Carolina	71
North Dakota	74
Ohio	74
Oklahoma	80
Oregon	82
Pennsylvania	83
South Carolina	85
Tennessee	85
Texas	88
Utah	103
Virginia	103
Washington	106
West Virginia	107
Wisconsin	109

INTRODUCTION

Currently published newspapers can be invaluable in researching your family's history. Using a newspaper published in or near the area where your ancestors lived, you may be able to contact people you could never locate otherwise - people who can give you priceless genealogical information.

There are three primary ways to get your genealogical problems mentioned in newspapers:

- by running an ad
- by a letter to the editor
- through the use of a special genealogical column

Each avenue offers some advantages and has some limitations.

The surest way is to pay for an ad. You are guaranteed publication, but you may be disappointed by the results. Your ad may be read by few people, unless you are willing to pay the price of a large ad that will really attract attention.

A more effective method of soliciting help is through a letter to the editor, because the letters are one of the most widely read features of a newspaper. However, there is no guarantee that your letter will be interesting enough to attract the editor's attention, or that space will be available. This prime space is usually in short supply.

The third method, and the best one when available, is the one explored in this book - genealogy columns. Such columns are read not only by genealogists, but by local history buffs, descendants of founding fathers (and mothers), and by many casual readers who may not be especially active in genealogy themselves.

Unfortunately, not every newspaper carries a genealogy column, so you need to do some preliminary research to locate them. That is the reason for this book - an attempt to list all the columns in publication prior to mid-1995. Both currently published and defunct columns are covered. A few "phantom" columns which have been reported to exist, but which in fact have never existed, are also identified to eliminate some wild goose chases!

This edition incorporates all the useful data in the previous publications: *Newspaper Genealogy Columns: A Preliminary Checklist* (1975) and *Newspaper Genealogical Column Directory* (1979), (1985), (1987), (1989), and (1992). Data is given here on nearly 125 verified columns appearing in almost 175 newspapers in over half the states, and several magazine columns. Geographic coverage spans the entire United States, and even Australia and Canada. These numbers do not reflect Miriam Weiner's ROOTS AND BRANCHES, which appears in 90 Jewish newspapers, and Myra Vanderpool Gormley's syndicated SHAKING YOUR FAMILY TREE, published throughout the United States.

Defunct columns contain a great deal of valuable genealogical data, and should be sought out where available. Even though they are no longer being printed, the old columns can often be found at the newspaper (if it is still in business), in a local library, genealogical society, historical society, or in the personal files of the editor of the column. It is common to find the columns have been indexed, or even published in book form. Information on back files, indexes, etc. is given in the listings where known.

The information presented here was obtained by surveys of the columnists. They were asked for the following data:

- (1) byline and address
- (2) research area (counties) covered
- (3) papers in which the column appears
- (4) frequency of the column
- (5) date the column was first published
- (6) requirements for a query
- (7) charge for a query
- (8) availability of back issues and indexes
- (9) publications sold by the columnist that pertain to the interest areas of the column
- (10) any other pertinent information
- (11) membership in the Council of Genealogy Columnists (CGC). *

Since complete information was not always provided, the listings given here are necessarily incomplete in many cases, but the data is presented in the format specified above using the same numerical codes. It is disappointing to see how few columns survive for more than a few years. The reason most frequently given for the demise of a column is that the columnist did not receive enough queries to justify its existence in the eyes of the newspaper management. This is a problem genealogists could easily solve by making more use of this medium!

When writing to a columnist, be sure to observe that columnist's requirements as you prepare your copy. If no requirements are specified, it is generally wise to type or print your query, keeping it short and to the point. Most columnists work on a volunteer basis and are not part of the newspaper's paid staff, so if you expect a reply, be sure to enclose the courtesy SASE (self-addressed stamped envelope).

Special thanks are due George Miller, as usual, for his assistance in this continuing quest. His efforts always make the Indiana listings the most accurate and current in the book. Thanks also to Margaret Ann Thetford and to Pat Mersereau, who were so generous in sharing update information on many of the columns. Thanks and a hug to daughter April Proffitt for the hours she spent laboriously proofreading the manuscript.

The compiler welcomes information about columns that have been missed. Additions and corrections should be sent to:

Anita Cheek Milner (619) 480-9130
910 Milane Lane 1 (800) 747-9130
Escondido, CA 92026 FAX: (619) 738-0405

NOTE: A "+" sign denotes columns that accept general queries.

* For further information about CGC, write 3607 Arlington, Lawton, OK 73505-6126.

MAGAZINES

Best Years reportedly features a genealogical column by Ann Cade, but the questionnaire was not returned. *Best Years* is published by NAMP (National Association of Mature People), 3018 North Sheridan Road, Chicago, IL 60657.

At one time, *Reminisce* featured TRACING ROOTS, a genealogical listing for paid subscribers, but the questionnaire was not returned. A sample copy of the magazine was available from 5927 Memory Lane, POB 3088, Milwaukee, WI 53201-3088.

Sharon DeBartolo Carmack, C.G.R.S., writes BRANCH OFFICE for the quarterly, *Reunions*. Contact her in care of the magazine, POB 11727, Milwaukee, WI 53211-0727.

Senior World, El Cajon, CA, no longer has a genealogy column.

Womens' Circle, 306 East Parr Road., Berne, IN 46711, will print paid queries, but has no genealogical column.

+(1) SWOPPER - GENEALOGICAL COLUMN, % *Yankee Magazine*, POB 520, Dublin, NH 03444. (2) The entire country. (3) *Yankee Magazine*. (4) 10-30 queries monthly. (5) 1935. (6) Queries can only pertain to people who lived before the 20th century. (7) Free. (8) Local libraries may have copies of Yankee Magazine.

MISCELLANEOUS COLUMNS

AFRICAN-AMERICAN RESEARCH

See Oakland County, Ml (3).

Marleta Childs' newspaper column, ROOT SEARCHING, has ceased publication. It appeared in the Lubbock, TX *West Texas Times* and the *Fort Worth Como Monitor*. Marleta Childs' column in *Family Records Today* ceased publication in 1995. The editors of *Family Records Today* were hoping to continue carrying a feature about African-American genealogy. Contact the society for more recent information. Nita Neblock, Editor-in-Chief, American Family Records Association, POB 15505, Kansas City, MO 64106. ROOT SEARCHING was indexed and is avaiiable in two volumes at $5.50 and $6.00 from Marleta Childs, POB 6825, Lubbock, TX 79493.

AUSTRALIAN RESEARCH

+ (1) FAMILY TREES by Miss Janet Reakes, POB 937, Hervey Bay, Queensland 4655, Australia. (2) All. (3) *Sunday Mail*, in State of Queensland and Northern New South Wales. (4) Weekly. (5) 1989. (6) None. (7) Free. (8) Columns have not been compiled and indexed by columnist. (9) Miss Reakes has numerous publications for sale. Contact her for a complete list. Of special interest is HOW TO TRACE YOUR CONVICT ANCESTORS.

Nick Vine Hall ceased writing his weekly YOU FOUND WHO IN YOUR FAMILY TREE? in 1990, after 187 issues. He now concentrates on radio work, i.e., GENEALOGICAL TALKBACK WITH NICK VINE HALL. Mr. Hall's column, which appeared in *The Land*, published in Richmond, New South Wales, covered research in New Zealand as well as Australia. Columns were not compiled and indexed, but copies of *The Land* are held by the City of Sydney Public Library, Pitt Street, Sydney, New South Wales 2000, Australia. Mr. Hall also has a full set of the columns. Contact Mr. Hall at 386 Ferrars Street, Albert Park, VIC 3206, AUSTRALIA, for further information about his radio show and his publications, including TRACING YOUR FAMILY HISTORY IN AUSTRALIA. Editor's Note: Please enclose an International Postal Reply Coupon when writing Mr. Hall. American postage cannot be used to mail a letter from Australia.

Nick Vine Hall also submitted the following information about another genealogy column:

Mrs. Cynthia Foley, 9 Smith Street, Dubbo, NSW 2830, Australia, has written WORD since 1991 for the *Orana Shopper/Daily Liberal*, Dubbo, NSW.

CANADIAN RESEARCH

See Penobscot Co., ME for a column that carries queries related to Maritime Canadian Provinces.

See Washington Co., ME for a column that carries queries related to Campobello, Deer Isle, and Western New Brunswick, Canada.

See Lauralee Clayton's column under **MAINE**, GENERAL, for a New Brunswick reference.

No response was received from F. E. McConvey, who reportedly writes IN-LAWS, OUTLAWS, & KINFOLKS, RR1 (Bayside), St. Andrews, New Brunswick, Canada EOG 2XO.

See Oakland Co., MI, for a column that carries queries related to Ontario, Canada.

See Spokane Co., WA for a column that carries queries related to western Canada.

(1) TRACING YOUR ROOTS by Ryan Taylor, *Kitchener Waterloo Record*, 225 Fairway Road South, Kitchener, Ontario, Canada N2G 4E5. (2) Western Ontario. (3) *Kitchener Waterloo Record*. (4) Tuesday. (5) March, 1993. (6) Queries not published. (8) Back columns available at Kitchener Public Library. (10) Column is not really local -- covers a broad spectrum of the genealogical world. Letters welcomed -- answered in column.

Brenda Merriam's column, GENEALOGY GAZETTE, which appeared in Ontario's *Early Canadian Life*, is no longer being published. It was published at 591 Argus Road, Oakville, Ontario, Canada L6J 3J4.

No response was received from Brian Gilchrist, whose column, TRACING YOUR ROOTS, was said to appear in Toronto's *Sunday Star*, 1 Yonge Street, Toronto, Canada M5E 1E6.

See Androscoggin, ME for a column that accepted Canadian-related queries, but which is no longer in publication.

COMPUTERS

(1) PAF 2.3 TOOLS & TECHNIQUES by Barbara Renick, 311 Copa De Oro Drive, Brea, CA 92621-7018. (2) Strictly the use of PAF genealogy software. (3) NGS CIG *Digest*. (4) Bi-monthly, in each newsletter. (5) May/June 1993 issue. (6) No queries.

COPYRIGHT

(1) COPYRIGHT CLARITY by Daniel J. Hay, 344 S. 500 W., Bountiful, UT 84010. (2) United States. (3) *Heritage Quest* magazine. (4) Bi-monthly. (5) September, 1993. (6) No queries. (8) Each issue is indexed, with a periodic cumulative index. (9) COPYRIGHT REFERENCE GUIDE, 4th Edition, Soft-cover. (11) Member of CGC.

FAMILY NAMES

(1) YOUR NAME by David L. Gold, *National Jewish Post and Opinion*, 2120 North Meridian St., Indianapolis, IN 46202-1373. (2) Jewish family names, Jewish given names, and Jewish genealogy. (3) *National Jewish Post and Opinion*. (4) Weekly. (5) 2 August 1989. (6) Booklet on the services of the Jewish Family Name File available for $1.00 + legal SASE with $.78 in *loose* US postage. (8) Columns now being compiled into a book. (9) JEWISH LANGUAGE REVIEW, 7 volumes, 1981-1987; JEWISH LINGUISTIC STUDIES, 2 volumes to date, 1989-1990. These two works contain much of onomastic and genealogical interest. Details available from address given above. Include SASE.

John C. Downing, who wrote KNOW YOUR NAME for several large newspapers, is deceased. His Sunday column appeared from 1965 until his death. The Collector's Book Shop, 15 South Fifth St., Richmond, VA 23219, might possibly have information on the location of the columns, but did not return the questionnaire.

Peter Carr reportedly writes a column for the *Excelsior*, a Spanish-language newspaper in Orange County, California and for *El Nuevo Patria*, in Miami, Florida, but a letter sent to him in San Bernardino, California was returned by the Postal Service, "Forwarding Order Expired." The weekly column was said to be sponsored by the Society of Hispanic Historical and Ancestral Research, with each column written about the origin of a particular Spanish surname. It was contemplated at one time that the column would also be distributed to English-language papers in Texas and in San Jose, California.

GENERAL RESEARCH

+(1) SHAKING YOUR FAMILY TREE by Myra Vanderpool Gormley, C.G., 8402 57th St. West, Tacoma, WA 98467-1638 (*Los Angeles Times* Syndicate). (2) Nationwide. (3) This column is syndicated nationally. It appears in *Los Angeles Times, Kansas City Times*, Portland *Oregonian*, and the Seattle *Post-Intelligencer*, as well as other newspapers in California, Washington, Nevada, Arizona, Massachusetts, Missouri, Florida, North Dakota, North Carolina, Oklahoma, Wisconsin, Utah, and Maryland. (4) weekly. (5) July 1983. (6) No queries. (8) Back columns not compiled and indexed. (11) Member of CGC.

Prodigy offers a Genealogy Bulletin Board. Myra Vanderpool Gormley, C.G., writes the weekly columns, usually about 500 to 600 words. Prodigy users can make hard copies of the columns and save them for later use. The columnist answers about 50 to 100 questions per week, ranging from beginner enquiries to more complex ones. She responds within two to three days. E-mail = VNBT04A@PRODIGY.COM.

No response was received from GENEALOGY WEEK, POB 90, Knightstown, IN 46148. Because this column started in 1968 and may still be in existence, the following information is reprinted from the fifth edition of NGCD: (2) Nationwide. There are no restrictions on locality of researching. (3) *AntiqueWeek*, in Central states and Eastern states. Column is same in both editions. Headquarters: Knightstown, IN 46118. (4) Weekly. (5) 1968. (6) Questions addressed to GENEALOGY SOURCES should be brief but indicate specific problem encountered in research. Staff cannot do research but will try to suggest new approaches to the problem. (7) No charge for GENEALOGY SOURCES questions, but there is a paid query column: $1.00 for 20 words; $0.10 for each additional word. (8) Back columns are indexed and on file in some libraries; bound copies of full newspaper at local library; microfilm at Indiana State Library. (9) The publisher, Mayhill Publications, Inc. carries history through The Bookmark, POB 90, Knightstown, IN 46148. (10) Names and addresses of persons writing to GENEALOGY SOURCES are not used, but letters are forwarded between interested parties when SASE is enclosed.

+(1) *Capper's*, 1503 S.W. 42nd St., Topeka, KS 66609-1265. (2) Entire United States. (3) *Capper 's*, Topeka, KS 66609-1265. (4) Every other week. (5) June, 1982. (6) *Capper 's* runs a genealogical classification in the Classified Advertising section of the paper. (7) $2.20 per word, 10 word minimum. (8) Back columns are at local [Topeka] library and may be indexed. (9) *Capper's* is $23.00 per year.

HERALDRY

See Palm Beach Co., FL.

Hazel Kraft Eilers' column, AT THE SIGN OF THE CREST, is no longer published. It appeared from January, 1953 to December, 1982. Copies of the columns are at Newberry Library, Chicago, IL and at Winnetka Public Library, Winnetka, IL.

IRISH RESEARCH

(1) Donn Devine, C.G., 2004 Kentmere Parkway, Wilmington, DE 19806-2014. (2) Ireland, Irish-American. (3) Philadelphia *Irish Edition*. (4) Monthly. (5) 1984. (6) Statement of research problem and objective (for discussion in column). (7) Free. (8) Topical index available from author (send long SASE). (11) Member of CGC.

At one time, GENEALOGICAL REVIEW appeared in *Irish Herald*, published in San Francisco, CA. The monthly column featured Irish names but was not compiled or indexed. It is possible that back issues of *Irish Herald* may be found in libraries.

JEWISH RESEARCH

See David L. Gold's YOUR NAME, under **FAMILY NAMES**.

(1) ROOTS AND BRANCHES by Miriam Weiner, C.G., 136 Sandpiper Key, Secaucus, NJ 07094. (2) Jewish genealogy and Holocaust research. (3) Column appears in over 90 Jewish newspapers throughout the United States. (4) Monthly. (5) September, 1986. (6) The column does not feature queries. (8) Back columns are accessible through request to the columnist. (9) Contact Miriam Weiner for a list of her numerous publications. (10) Contact Miriam Weiner for a list of her extensive qualifications as both a writer and national lecturer. Co-editor of THE ENCYCLOPEDIA OF JEWISH GENEALOGY, Volume 1. (11) Member of CGC.

NATIVE AMERICAN

OTTAWA/MIAMI: See Paulding Co., OH.

REGIONAL UNITED STATES

GULF COAST: See Mobile Co., AL & Jackson Co., MS.

MIDWEST: See GENERAL, UT.

NEW ENGLAND: See Androscoggin Co., ME for a column that accepted New England-related queries, but which is no longer in publication. See Penobscot Co., ME for a column that is still active.

See also GENERAL, CT, for information on a column that appeared from 1934 to 1967 in the Hartford Times.

PACIFIC NORTHWEST: See Spokane Co. WA.

SOUTH: See SOUTHERN ROOTS, under Escambia Co., FL, Caddo Parish, LA, Harris Co., TX, & GENERAL, UT.

WEST

(1) TRAILS GROW DIM, Western Publications, POB 2107, Stillwater, OK 74076. (2) The publisher accepts inquiries about ancestors and relatives who lived and died during the OLD WEST period of 1880-1910. Anything more recent than that is considered a missing person item and will not be run. (4) The column appears

monthly in *True West* and quarterly in *Old West*. (5) Circa 1967. (6) Inquiries should be kept to under 150 words. (7) Free. (8) An index through 1979 is $7.95.

SCOTTISH RESEARCH

A. MAXIM COPPAGE's column, SEARCHING FOR SCOTTISH ANCESTORS, may still appear in *The Highlander*, but his questionnaire was not returned. *The Highlander* address: POB 397, Barrington, IL 60011.

COLUMNS ARRANGED BY STATE

ALABAMA

GENERAL: See Jefferson Co., AL, Plaquemines Parish, LA & Jackson Co., MS.

CENTRAL ALABAMA: See Bibb Co., AL.

SOUTHEASTERN ALABAMA: See Thomas Co., GA.

SOUTHERN ALABAMA: See Choctaw Co., AL.

BALDWIN COUNTY: See Mobile Co., AL.

BIBB COUNTY

(1) LOST AND FOUND ANCESTORS by Elia G. Daws, POB 73, *Centreville Press*, Centreville, AL 35042. (2) Bibb, Perry, Shelby, Chilton, Tuscaloosa counties in Alabama, or any central Alabama county. (3) *Centreville Press*, Centreville, AL; Marion *Times-Standard*, Perry County, AL. (4) Weekly. (5) 1979. (6) None. (7) Free. (8) Back columns are at the Brent/Centreville Library. (9) BIBB COUNTY, AL, 1860 CENSUS, arranged alphabetically, $11.00; KEMPER COUNTY, MS, 1850 CENSUS, $11.00; KEMPER COUNTY, MS, 1860 CENSUS, $11.00; PERRY COUNTY, AL, 1850 CENSUS, indexed, $11.00; PERRY COUNTY, AL, 1860, CENSUS, indexed, $13.50. All prices postpaid.

BLOUNT COUNTY

(1) LINEAGE AND LETTERS by Mrs. Emma Linder, Cherry Hill Farm, *Blount Countian*, POB 310, Oneonta, AL 35121. (2) Alabama counties, especially Blount, St. Clair, Etowah, Marsh, Cullman, and Jefferson. (3) *Blount Countian*, Oneonta, AL. (4) Weekly. (5) 22 February 1978. (6) Queries must be written. (7) Free. (8) Not all columns are indexed. Clipped columns are in looseleaf form in Genealogy Collection in Blount County Memorial (historical) Museum in Oneonta, Alabama. (9) No publications for sale. Columnist may make copies of requested materials.

CALHOUN COUNTY: See Saint Clair Co., AL.

CHAMBERS COUNTY: See Troup Co., GA.

CHEROKEE COUNTY

TRACING SOUTHERN FAMILIES by Mrs. Frank Ross Stewart, Sr., appeared weekly in the *Cherokee County Herald*, Centre, AL 35960 and the *Anniston Star*, Anniston, AL 36201. The editor passed away, and the column may have been canceled. The questionnaire was not returned. Queries and gleanings from Mrs. Stewart's columns appeared in each issue of *American Genealogy*, POB 1587,

Stephenville, TX 76401. There were no limitations on queries. When Mrs. Stewart was writing the column, her address was: c/o The Southern Society of Genealogists, POB 295, Centre, AL 35960.

CHILTON COUNTY: See Bibb Co., AL.

CHOCTAW COUNTY

(1) Tommy Campbell, Editor, *The Choctaw Advocate*, POB 475, Butler, AL 36904. (2) Choctaw, Marengo, Washington, and Sumter counties, in Alabama; most counties in southern Alabama; Lauderdale, Clark, and Wayne counties, Mississippi; some Georgia, South Carolina, and North Carolina areas. (3) *The Choctaw Advocate*, Butler, AL. (4) Monthly. (5) 1979. (6) Should be typed or plainly printed, as brief as possible, and include writer's name, address and (optional) phone number. (7) Free to subscribers; $5.00 to non-subscribers, 50-word limit, $.20 per word over 50. (8) Back columns are at Choctaw County Public Library, 124 N. Academy St., Butler, AL 36904. Attn: Ann H. Gay. (9) A subscription to the newspaper is $25.00 a year. (10) The paper will also review genealogical books. Send a copy of the book along with any pertinent data. "Our paper is read by 14,000 readers in 27 states. We get good response to queries."

CULLMAN COUNTY: See Blount Co., AL.

DALLAS COUNTY

Apparently the *Selma News Record* carries no genealogy column.

ETOWAH COUNTY: See Blount Co., AL.

JACKSON COUNTY

Christine Sumner's THEY PASSED THIS WAY is no longer published in the Scottsboro *Daily Sentinel*. The Scottsboro library may have copies of the column, which appeared around 1975.

JEFFERSON COUNTY: See Blount Co., AL.

(1) FAMILY TIES, *The Birmingham News*, POB 2553, Birmingham, AL 35202. (2) State of Alabama. (3) *The Birmingham News*, in the "Lifestyle" section. (4) Weekly, on Sunday. (5) About 1993. (7) Free. (8) Back columns have not been compiled and indexed for reader reference, but may be accessible in the Southern History Department of the Birmingham Public Library.

MARENGO COUNTY: See Choctaw Co., AL.

MARSH COUNTY: See Blount Co., AL.

MOBILE COUNTY

(1) CLIMBING THE FAMILY TREE by Eugenia Parker, POB 9136, Mobile, AL 36691. (2) Mobile and Baldwin counties, AL; Gulf Coast. (3) *Mobile Press Register* ("Suburban People"). (4) Weekly. (5) 1980. (6) Send SASE to columnist for detailed instructions on submitting a query. (7) Free. (8) Columns are available at the Mobile Public Library, in the Local History and Genealogy Division (newspapers on microfilm), by date. Beginning with the year 1989, and thereafter, columns are being compiled and indexed, with 1989 and 1990 columns available now. (10) Typed queries are preferable. At the very least they should be legible. Columnist will not spend any time trying to decipher illegible handwriting. If an answer is requested, or any communication, SASE is essential. A photocopy of the column in which a query appears costs $1.00 in advance. NOTE: This column replaced TITLES AND TALES, whose author, Ruth Warren, died in June, 1980. Another column, HERITAGE AND HISTORY, carries no queries. (11) Member of CGC.

MONTGOMERY COUNTY

ROOTS & RECORDS reportedly appears in the Sunday *Montgomery Advertiser-Alabama Journal*, POB 1000, Montgomery, AL 36101-1000, but the questionnaire was not returned.

MORGAN COUNTY

Louise Milam Julich's SOUTHERN KINFOLKS is no longer published in Decatur's *Morgan County Free Press*. Lilla Brackeen's HUNTING ANCESTORS is not carried by Decatur's *River City News*. Back issues of both weekly columns may be in the Decatur library.

PERRY COUNTY: See Bibb Co., AL.

RANDOLPH COUNTY: See Troup Co., GA.

SAINT CLAIR COUNTY: See Blount Co., AL.

(1) TREE CLIMBING -- GENEALOGY AND HISTORY OF ST. CLAIR COUNTY by Charlene Simpson, c/o Ashville Museum & Archives, POB 187, Ashville, AL 35953. (2) St. Clair, Shelby, Talladega, and Calhoun counties. (3) *St. Clair News Aegis*. (4) Twice a month; weekly, when there are enough queries. (5) March, 1992. (6) There is currently no length restriction. Use good judgment. Queries are printed essentially as they are received, edited only for clarity and format. In the event of errors on the part of the columnist or the newspaper, a corrected query will be run in a later edition. No further liability is assumed for errors. (7) Free. (8) Columns have been compiled but not indexed. They are available at the Ashville Museum & Archives. (9) Ashville Museum & Archives sells several publications about St. Clair County. Send SASE for the list. (10)

Family history books may be submitted for review, after which they are donated to the Ashville Museum & Archives, unless accompanied by return postage.

SHELBY COUNTY: See Bibb Co. & Saint Clair Co, AL.

SUMTER COUNTY: See Choctaw Co., AL.

TALLADEGA COUNTY: See Saint Clair Co., AL.

TUSCALOOSA COUNTY: See Bibb Co., AL.

WASHINGTON COUNTY: See Choctaw Co., AL.

ARKANSAS

GENERAL: See Hancock Co., KY.

NORTH CENTRAL ARKANSAS: See Howell Co., MO.

NORTHEASTERN ARKANSAS: See Ripley Co., MO.

NORTHWESTERN ARKANSAS: See Benton Co., AR, Union Co., AR, Washington Co., AR, & McDonald Co., MO.

OZARKS: See Newton Co., MO.

SOUTHEASTERN ARKANSAS: See Ashley Co., AR.

WESTERN ARKANSAS: See LeFlore Co., OK.

ASHLEY COUNTY

Blanche Turlington no longer writes KIN KOLLECTING for Ashley County Genealogical Society, P.O. Drawer R, Crossett, AR 71635, and there has been no replacement. The monthly column covered research in southeastern Arkansas and had appeared in the *Ashley County Ledger* and the *Ashley News Observer* since February, 1986. First three years were indexed and available at Paul Sullins Library, Crossett, AR. (9) ASHLEY COUNTY 1880 CENSUS, $15.00; ASHLEY COUNTY MARRIAGES, 1849-1910, 1 volume, $20.00; ASHLEY COUNTY TAX LIST, 1890, $7.50.

BENTON COUNTY

(1) BACK PEDALING by Raymond E. Jefferies, Jeff-Gen Research, POB 369, Pea Ridge, AR 72751-1369. (2) Benton Co. and some Washington Co. (3) Two newspapers merged into one now called *The Morning News of Northwest Arkansas*, sent to Rogers, AR in Benton Co., and Springdale, AR in Washington Co. (4)

Every Sunday. (5) 14 April 1991. (6) Benton County references. If too long, query may be run in continuing columns. More than one query may be sent, but all may not be printed at one time. (7) Free. (8) Back columns may be compiled and indexed and published. (10) Columnist not able to take on individual research at this time, but column will be continued. Columnist prints very brief book reviews or other publications, only as space permits. Announcements of family gatherings published at columnist's discretion.

(1) OZARK ORIGINS by Nadean Riley Bell, 1205 Northwest 11th, Bentonville, AR 72712-4119. (2) Benton Co. and the surrounding area. (3) *Benton County Daily Record*, Bentonville, AR 72712. (4)Weekly. (5) September, 1992. (6) 75 words or less. Include name and address. Send to the columnist at the address given in (1). (7) Free. (8) Back columns not compiled and indexed for reader reference.

BRADLEY COUNTY

Until his death in 1982, Robert Gatewood wrote a genealogical column. The Bradley County Historical Society, Warren, AR 71671, may have copies of the column.

CLEVELAND COUNTY

Harold D. Sadler's weekly column, FOOTPRINTS ON THE SANDS OF TIME, no longer appears in the *Cleveland County Herald*. The columns were published from August, 1967, but were not compiled and indexed. Copies were available only in the files of the *Cleveland County Herald*. The column was largely about people and their living conditions in the past. Court and marriage records were published. Events of 50, 75, and 100 years ago were reprinted.

CRAWFORD COUNTY

(1) RIVER VALLEY ROOTS by Nadean Riley Bell, 1205 Northwest 11th, Bentonville, AR 72712-4119. (2) Crawford Co. and the surrounding areas. (3) *The Press Argus-Courier*, 100 No. 11th, Van Buren, AR 72956. (4) Weekly, as space available. (5) September, 1992. (6) 75 words or less. Include name and address. Send to the columnist at the address given in (1). (7) Free. (8) See (9). Copies accessible at Crawford County Genealogical Society, Alma, AR; Fort Smith (AR) Public Library; and Fayetteville (AR) Public Library. (9) RIVER VALLEY ROOTS, 1992-1994, $15.00, plus $3.00 postage and handling. Available from the columnist at the address given in (1).

DREW COUNTY

There apparently is no genealogy column in the *Advance Monticellonian*.

FRANKLIN COUNTY

The following column was canceled February, 1995:

(1) FRANKLIN FAMILY FOLK by Nadean Riley Bell, 1205 Northwest 11th, Bentonville, AR 72712-4119. (2) Franklin Co. and the surrounding area. (3) Column appeared in *The Spectator*, Ozark, AR 72949. (4) Weekly, as space available. (5) September, 1992 - January, 1995. (8) See (9). Copies accessible at Ozark (AR) Public Library; Fort Smith (AR) Public Library; and Fayetteville (AR) Public Library. (9) FRANKLIN FAMILY FOLK, 1992-1995, $15.00, plus $3.00 postage and handling. Available from the columnist at the address given in (1).

GARLAND COUNTY

DEAR MRS. CLINE: GENEALOGICAL NEWSPAPER COLUMN FROM THE HOT SPRINGS NEWS, 1968-1979, by Inez E. Cline. This book included historical articles, many genealogical queries with answers, tips for researching ancestors in Arkansas, reunions, seminars, meetings, and other valuable information. At one time it was available from McDowell Publications, 11129 Pleasant Ridge Road, Utica, KY 42376, but is probably out of print.

LAWRENCE COUNTY

There has *never* been a genealogy column in the Walnut Ridge *Times Dispatch*.

MILLER COUNTY: See Bowie Co., TX.

PULASKI COUNTY

GRASS ROOTS by Margaret Ross appeared in the *Arkansas Gazette* from 22 February 1979 until the columnist's retirement on 1 September 1984. The *Gazette*, which is published in Little Rock, now has no genealogy column. The Little Rock Public Library has a complete file of the columns, and other Arkansas libraries are also reported to have them.

SALINE COUNTY

Carolyn Earle Billingsley's SALINE RESEARCH no longer appears in the *Benton Courier*. It may appear sporadically in the future. Contact the columnist at 2301 Billingsley Lane, Alexander, AR 72002. The newspaper is available on microfilm at the Arkansas History Commission (State Archives).

UNION COUNTY

THE GENIE TRAIL by Helen Dunn, is no longer being published. It appeared in The *El Dorado-News Times*, El Dorado, AR, monthly or semi-monthly from January, 1987. The final date of publication wasn't given in the columnist's response. In addition to queries, the column featured how-to's for beginning genealogists and information on upcoming seminars. Copies of the column may be available at the Barton Library, 200 East 5th, El Dorado, AR 71730.

WASHINGTON COUNTY: See Benton Co., AR.

(1) RELATIVITY by Gene and Mary Jo Godfrey, POB 964, West Fork, AR 72774. (2) Washington Co. (3) *Northwest Arkansas Times* (Sunday), Fayetteville, AR; *Lincoln Leader* (Thursday), Lincoln, AR; *Prairie Grove Enterprise* (Thursday), Prairie Grove, AR. (4) Weekly. (5) September, 1991. (6) Up to 75 words, plus submitter's name and address. Phone number optional. (7) Free. (8) Table of contents has been compiled. Columnists working on index. Available in Grace Keith Genealogical Collection, Fayetteville Public Library, 217 E. Dickson, Fayetteville, AR 72701.

WHITE COUNTY

The *Searcy Daily Citizen* has no genealogy column.

CALIFORNIA

GENERAL: See Kern Co., CA & Los Angeles Co., CA.

MOTHER LODE COUNTRY: See Amador Co., CA.

AMADOR COUNTY

PEDIGREE PROSPECTOR, which appeared weekly in the *Amador Dispatch*. Back columns would be available only through back issues of the newspaper, published in Jackson, CA 95642. No other information was given about this column.

IMPERIAL COUNTY

There has never been a genealogy column in the El Centro newspaper.

KERN COUNTY

(1) ANCESTOR AMBLING by Ann McDanell, 2328 Oleander, Delano, CA 93215. (2) Kern and Tulare counties. (3) (Delano) *Record, Arvin Tiller, Lamont Reporter, Shafter Press, Wasco Tribune*. (4) Monthly. (5) 1988. (6) Query should be approximately 50 words, with a California connection, surnames capitalized and contain a name, date, and place. (7) Free. (8) A booklet of the back columns is with the Kern County Library System. It has a table of contents and a query index. The booklet is also available from the columnist. (11) Member of CGC.

LOS ANGELES COUNTY: See Orange Co., CA (10).

The *Long Beach Independent Press Telegram* carries no genealogy column.

The questionnaire to GENEALOGY BEGINS WITH U was not returned. Information from the fifth edition of NGCD is listed below, but the column may no longer be in publication:

+(1) GENEALOGY BEGINS WITH U, *California Intermountain News*, 6708 Melrose Ave., Los Angeles, CA 90038. (2) California and anywhere. (3) *California Intermountain News*. (4) Weekly. (5) October, 1982. (6) Queries should be directed to the paper. They are then forwarded to Michael Cunningham in Gilmer, TX, who writes the column. (7) Free. (8) Back columns not compiled and indexed. (9) A subscription to the paper is $4.95 a year. The column is 3/4 page of an 8-page paper. (10) The paper is aimed at the Latter Day Saint reader, but general readers are welcome to submit queries.

MENDOCINO COUNTY

Ruth Eshelman's questionnaire was not returned. She wrote a weekly column for the *Mendocino Beacon* from 1979-1984. The columns covered the entire gamut of research. She reprinted the columns in a 300-page paperback, which sold for $11.00, including postage and handling. The book was printed on acid-free paper, with an added index. The most recent address found for Ruth Eshelman was 18170 N. 91st Ave., Apt. 1181, Peoria, AZ 85382-0869, but that may no longer be valid.

ORANGE COUNTY

+(1) GENEALOGY by Georgia Dent, POB 11626, Santa Ana, CA 92711. (2) Anywhere inside *or* outside U.S. (3) Accent, *Orange County Register*, Santa Ana, CA. (4) Bi-weekly. (5) October, 1990. (6) Send SASE if you live outside newspaper's circulation area. Submit queries only -- no meeting announcements or books for review. (7) Free. (8) Orange County Genealogical Society has clippings, but no index. (10) This is a question-and-answer research column. Missing relative queries are also accepted, if person(s) lived or could be living in Los Angeles or Orange counties. (11) Member of CGC.

SAN BENITO COUNTY

It is reported that Annette Lutnesky Perry, MLS, writes a bi-weekly genealogy column for the *Miracle Miles* newspaper, circulation about 35,000, which is distributed in Morgan Hill, Gilroy, and Hollister. Annette Perry is a member of CGC and her address is 1841 Nora Drive, Hollister, CA 95023.

SAN DIEGO COUNTY

The El Cajon *Daily Californian* carries no genealogy column.

Senior World of El Cajon no longer runs Jill Rueble Hughes' YOUR FAMILY HISTORY. No other information was available. *Senior World's* address is POB 1565, El Cajon, CA 92022.

Now being broadcast in San Diego at KSDO 1130 AM news talk radio on Saturdays, from 6:00 to 7:00 p.m., PST, a radio program, THE FAMILY HISTORIAN [Trademark symbol], Climbing the Family Tree with Brad York. Listeners are encouraged to call with questons dealing with genealogy, family history, ancestral research, or tracing lineage. Phone: (619) 669-1130.

SAN JOAQUIN COUNTY

A letter to Jewel Dixon Johnson's GENEALOGY CORNER, in Manteca, was returned by the Postal Service, "Forwarding Time Expired." A letter to Lodi was also returned by the Postal Service.

SANTA CLARA COUNTY: See San Benito Co., CA.

SHASTA COUNTY

DIGGING AND CLIMBING is no longer carried in the *Anderson Press*, 2995 East St., Anderson, CA 96007. No other information was given.

STANISLAUS COUNTY

There is no genealogy column in Hughson.

TULARE COUNTY: See Kern Co., CA.

CONNECTICUT

GENERAL

(1) THE HARTFORD TIMES DEPARTMENT OF GENEALOGY (later changed to GENEALOGICAL OUESTIONS AND ANSWERS) by Bertha Lee (Hempstead) Benn and Louise (Benn) MacNeely. (2) Connecticut and New England. (3) *The Hartford Times*. (4) Weekly, on Saturday. (5) 27 January 1934 - 1960 by Bertha Lee (Hempstead) Benn; 1960 - 29 May 1967 by Louise (Benn) MacNeely. Louise MacNeely took over the column at her mother's death in 1960 and wrote it until her own retirement in 1967. (8) The columns from June 1940 through 1956 have been reproduced in microfiche with a complete surname and given name index as the *Marion Donoghue Combination*. This 23-fiche work may be available from Genealogical Society of South Brevard County, Florida, Inc., POB 786, Melbourne, FL 32902-0786, as well as in larger Connecticut libraries. A microcard version also exists for 1957 through to the final column in 1967, and is available at the Rhode Island Historical Society Library, Providence; and New London Public

Library. An annual surname-only index appears with this version. Editor's Note: The above information was sent to me by Frederick C. Hart Jr., C.G., in his excellent article, The Hartford Times Genealogical Column, which appeared in the February, 1993 issue of *Connecticut Ancestry*. I recommend reading his article in its entirety. Of special interest was Mr. Hart's reference to Mrs. Benn's obituary, which mentioned that "she had patterned her column after one which had appeared earlier in the Times, 'until World War I.'" Mr. Hart may investigate this column in a future article.

HARTFORD COUNTY

A questionnaire to Charles H. Copeland, 55 Windbrook Drive, Windsor, CT 06095-3562 was not returned.

DISTRICT OF COLUMBIA

The questionnaire to the *Washington Post* was not returned, but it is believed the information given in the fifth edition of NGCD is still fairly accurate, so that listing is repeated below:

The *Washington Post* carries a special monthly page on GENEALOGY in the Sunday Classified Announcements & Notices Section, which started 28 October 1984. This page is designed to keep pace with the advertisers' and readers' needs by putting at the fingertips of readers a wealth of genealogy information such as Ancestral Queries (for ancestors born at least 100 years ago), Genealogy Supplies, Services, Books, Magazines, Family Reunion Announcements, Organizations, and Misc. Items. The Sunday *Post* has over two million readers. For more info call Liz Stevenson, Classified Advertising Rep. at 1 (800) 624-2367, Ext. 7031; or write to her c/o *Post*, 1150 15th St. NW, Washington, DC 20071.

FLORIDA

GENERAL

+(1) FOOTPRINTS INTO THE PAST by Brian Michaels, POB 1305, Palatka, FL 32178-1305. (2) Not restricted by topic or area, but queries concerning Florida most desired. (3) *Florida Living* magazine. (4) Monthly. (5) May, 1984. (6) Prefer 50-word maximum; three queries per submission maximum. (7) Free. (8) Columns are accessible at the Palatka Public Library, Putnam County Library System. They will be incorporated into a forthcoming volume, with the working title of THE JOYS OF GENEALOGY, published in 1995. Address any queries regarding this volume to Brian Michaels at the address given above. (11) Member of CGC.

NORTHERN FLORIDA: See Thomas Co., GA.

ALACHUA COUNTY

YOUR FAMILY TREE by Gene and Elaine May has not been published since about 1988. It appeared weekly from May, 1977 in the *Gainesville Sun*, P.O. Drawer A, Gainesville, FL 32602. The column varied from very general reader interest articles to information regarding specific names found in the southeastern United States, in addition to queries. Gene and Elaine May also collected humorous and unusual epitaphs. At one time, it was planned to compile and index the columns, but no further information was available.

CHARLOTTE COUNTY

ROOTS, BY ROXANNE is no longer published in the *Charlotte Sun*, Fort Charlotte, and the columns were not compiled and indexed. Back issues of the column may be in the library at Fort Charlotte, FL 33952.

COLLIER COUNTY

Charles Guarino's WHAT'S IN YOUR NAME? is no longer syndicated by the Field Syndicate. No other information was received.

DUVAL COUNTY

After 17 years, LaViece Smallwood ceased writing OUT ON A LIMB. At one time, her weekly column, which was international in scope, was carried in the *Florida Times-Union* (from 1978) and the *Idaho Post Register* (from 1984). She printed free queries, if they were typed. Back columns had not been compiled and indexed. LaViece Smallwood's address: POB 1800, *Idaho Falls Register*, Idaho Falls, ID 83403.

It is reported that CGC member Beth Gay is writing HUNTING FORBEARS for Jacksonville's *Times-Union* and the *Moultrie Observer*.

ESCAMBIA COUNTY

FAMILY QUEST by Dot Brown was published from November, 1981 to 1993. It was reportedly being indexed by the West Florida Genealogical Society. Back columns are on file at Pensacola Historical Society, 405 S. Adams St., Pensacola, FL 32501. The column covered everything of interest to genealogists -- book reviews, queries, notices of conventions and workshops, etc. It covered any area. FAMILY QUEST was replaced by the following column:

(1) SOUTHERN ROOTS by Janice B. Palmer, % Life Section, *Pensacola News Journal*, POB 12710, Pensacola, FL 32574. (2) All Southern states, and other states relating to migration of families to the South. (3) *Pensacola News Journal*. (4) Weekly, in Sunday's Life Section. (5) December, 1993. (6) Queries are accepted for announcements of conventions and family reunions, book reviews,

research tips, new software and technology, self-publishing, seeking families who migrated to the South, local history, etc. (7) Free. (8) Back columns are accessible at the Pensacola Public Library. Also, each anniversary the past year's columns are printed in book form and are available from the writer. Cost is $10.00 plus $2.50 shipping and handling. Order from Janice B. Palmer, 6302 Fairview Drive, Pensacola, FL 32505-2057. (9) SOUTHERN ROOTS, Volume I is 68 pp. with index by subject, book, name, location, etc.; Volume II is 63 pp. with full index. Soft-cover, plastic-comb binding. (11) Member of CGC.

HILLSBOROUGH COUNTY

The questionnaire to the Florida Genealogical Society, Inc., POB 18424, Tampa, FL 33679-8624 was not returned. Its monthly column, GENEALOGY, which began publication on 19 August 1990 in the Tampa Tribune, did not accept queries. The column gave information on how to start research, sources, etc. Back columns had been compiled and indexed for reader reference. The Society published 8 volumes of cemetery records for Hillsborough County. Those books may still be available. Contact the Society at the address given above.

LAKE COUNTY: See Sumter Co., FL.

OSCEOLA COUNTY

THE FLORIDA SEARCH apparently only appeared in the *Saint Cloud News*, POB 578, Saint Cloud, FL 32769, from 1978 to 1980. No other information was available.

PALM BEACH COUNTY

The questionnaire to The Baron of Drumtariff, 381 Churchill Road, West Palm Beach, FL 33405 was not returned. The weekly column, THE HERALD, was local, national, and international in scope. It was concerned mainly with items of a heraldry theme and nature, especially as related to genealogy, and appeared in the *Palm Beacher* beginning June, 1989. Back columns are available at West Palm Beach libraries.

SUMTER COUNTY

(1) KINSEEKERS CORNER by Jeannette Phethean, 19 Quail Run, Wildwood, FL 34785. (2) Lake and Sumter counties, but columnist does have queries from many other areas of the country. (3) *Leesburg Commercial*, Leesburg, FL. (4) Bi-weekly, on Monday. (5) 1980. (6) Letter to the columnist, plus SASE, so that columnist may forward any replies made to her. (7) Free. (8) Columns have not been compiled and indexed for reader reference, but are available on microfilm of newspaper in the Leesburg Library. Columnist also retains her personal collection of the columns.

GEORGIA

GENERAL: See Choctaw Co., AL & Dougherty Co., GA.

NORTHEASTERN GEORGIA: See De Lay's column under Fulton Co., GA & Hall Co., GA.

SOUTHERN GEORGIA: See Thomas Co., GA.

SOUTHWESTERN GEORGIA: See Dougherty Co., GA.

BALDWIN COUNTY: See Dougherty Co., GA.

BANKS COUNTY: See De Lay's column under Fulton Co., GA.

BULLOCH COUNTY: See Screven Co., GA.

BURKE COUNTY: See Jefferson Co., GA & Screven Co., GA.

CARROLL COUNTY

There is no genealogy column in Carrollton.

CATOOSA COUNTY

Dr. Dan Whitaker no longer writes HISTORICAL NOTEBOOK FOR NORTHWEST GEORGIA, covering Catoosa and Walker counties. Judy L. Reed, Corresponding Secretary of the Catoosa County Historical Society, POB 113, Ringgold, GA 30736, reports there is presently no one to write a column for the paper. There are plans by President Elaine E. Taylor to have members contributing to the *Catoosa County News* and some to the *Chattanooga* (Tennessee) *Free Press*.

CLARKE COUNTY: See De Lay's column under Fulton Co., GA.

There is no FAMILY TREE CORNER in the *Athens Daily News*.

CLAYTON COUNTY

Elizabeth Alligood's weekly column is no longer published. It covered Clayton, Crawford, Mitchell, and Pike counties. The columns may be available at the Riverdale Library.

COLUMBIA COUNTY: See Jefferson Co., GA.

Janette S. Kelley's column ran from 1979 to 1985 and covered research in Columbia and McDuffie counties. No other information about the column was available.

COWETA COUNTY

(1) TREETOPS TO ROOTS by Mrs. R.T. Gunby, 8031 Hwy. 54, Sharpsburg, GA 30277. (2) Coweta County and international. There are subscribers throughout the states and interest is widespread. (3) *The Newnan Times-Herald*, POB 1052, Newnan, GA 30264. (4) Bi-weekly. (5) July, 1980. (6) Type or print queries; 50-word maximum. Coweta County has preference. Others, as space allows. (7) Free. Expect to exchange material. (8) Columns compiled in scrapbook at Coweta County Research Center. (9) *Coweta County Genealogical Society Quarterly*, $15.00 a year (about 100 pages); contact columnist about COWETA COUNTY CEMETERY BOOK and COWETA CENSUS. Newnan-Coweta Historical Society, Inc., POB 1001, Newnan, GA 30264, also has Coweta County publications. Send for descriptive flyer. (10) Lineage charts and family group sheets accepted and placed in local Coweta County Research Center. Columnist will also review gift books, after which they are placed in the genealogical collection.

CRAWFORD COUNTY: See Clayton Co., GA.

DOUGHERTY COUNTY

(1) KNOWING YOUR ANCESTORS by Marie De Lamar, 1006 Sixth Ave., Albany, GA 31701. (2) All Georgia, but newspaper is distributed in southwestern Georgia. (3) *Albany Herald*. (4) Monthly, the third Sunday. "Paper under new management and we have AP and UP columns coming from all directions. Local columnists (about 5) are only accepted once a month now." (5) 29 October 1972. (6) Queries must be related to Georgia. (7) Free. (8) Back columns not compiled or indexed. (9) Remaining stock of columnist's books have been turned over to Boyd Publishers, Millegeville, GA, for sale: 1830 CENSUS OF GEORGIA INDEX; RECORDS OF BALDWIN COUNTY, GEORGIA; CEDED LANDS (Wilkes County, Georgia). (10) The columnist does professional genealogical research in southwestern Georgia.

EFFINGHAM COUNTY: See Screven Co., GA.

ELBERT COUNTY: See Hart Co., GA.

FANNIN COUNTY

Leroy Weese's local history column is no longer published in Blue Ridge's *Summit Post*. All back issues of the newspaper are filed in the Office of the Probate Judge, Fannin County Courthouse, Clerk of Court, Blue Ridge, GA 30513. Records can be searched in person. No other information was available.

FAYETTE COUNTY

Varney Graves' VIGNETTES OF HISTORY is no longer published in the *Fayette County News*, POB 96, Fayetteville, GA 30214, and back issues are not available. The Fayetteville library may have back columns.

Joel Dixon Wells no longer publishes a genealogy column in Hampton.

FORSYTH COUNTY

HERITAGE SHARING by Donna Parrish is no longer published in the *Forsyth County News*, Cumming, GA 30130. Copies of the column may be available in the Cumming library.

FRANKLIN COUNTY: See Hart Co., GA.

FULTON COUNTY

The questionnaire to Marie De Lay was not returned. However, her columns had been in publication for so long that the information from the fifth edition of NGCD is given below:

(1) FAMILY TREES and OUR ANCESTORS (two columns) by Marie De Lay, 1775 Alvarado Terrace, SW, Atlanta, GA 30310. (2) OUR ANCESTORS covers Madison County and northeast Georgia. FAMILY TREES primarily covers Jackson County, but also Banks, Clarke, Madison, Walton, and Habersham counties. (3) FAMILY TREES, *Jackson Herald/Banks County News*, Jefferson, GA 30549; OUR ANCESTORS, *The Comer News and Danielsville Monitor*. (4) OUR ANCESTORS appears weekly; FAMILY TREES is published infrequently. (6) No specific query requirements, but long queries are edited. Jackson and Madison counties adjoin, and a part of Jackson was included when Madison was created in 1811. (7) Free. (8) OUR ANCESTORS, which began publication in February, 1978, is now available in book form. The index contains over 3500 surnames, names of churches, cemeteries, towns, etc. The columns cover a variety of subjects: helpful suggestions and sources for family research, Bible records, cemetery recordings, census records, wills, personal family stories, book reviews, etc. The book is $16.00 from Marie De Lay at the address given in (1). (9) MISCELLANEOUS RECORDS OF JACKSON CO., GA 1790-1859, compiled and published by Joseph T. Maddox and Mary Carter, paperback, 66 pp. with 18 pp. index, $8.00 postpaid, from Marie De Lay at the address given in (1). The columnist's supply of FAMILY TREE indexes, which covered 283 columns from March, 1972 to October, 1978 is out of print, and she has no plans to reprint it. Copies are at the Georgia Archives, Georgia Genealogical Society, and Atlanta Public Library, as well as many other libraries around the country. The columnist's index to Frary Elrod's HISTORICAL NOTES ON JACKSON COUNTY, GA is available for $3.00 from Jackson County Historical Society, Jefferson, GA 30549. The book is available from Mrs. Elrod at Rt. 1, POB 262, Jefferson, GA 30549.

(1) GENEALOGY by Kenneth H. Thomas, Jr., POB 901, Decatur, GA 30031. E-mail address (at home) -- KTOMJR@aol.com. (2) Column covers mostly Georgia books, but does mention things of real interest in nearby states such as North and South Carolina, and Alabama, visits to archives in other states, and national issues. (3) *The Atlanta Journal* and *The Atlanta Constitution*, POB 4689, Atlanta, GA 30302. (4) From 1977 to 1983, weekly; from 1983 to 1988, monthly; from 1988, twice a month; since September, 1994, weekly. Column appears in Sunday's Dixie Living Section. Circulation of Sunday edition is 650,000. (5) 7 May 1977. (6) No queries. (7) Research questions on a topic may be considered. (8) Copies of the columns are kept by many libraries, including Georgia Department of Archives and History. (9) The columns from 1977 and 1978 were compiled in book form and are available from Mr. Thomas at the address given in (1). The book, KEN THOMAS ON GENEALOGY is hardbound, 200 pp., contains a comprehensive index, and is $23.75 (plus sales tax where applicable). (10) Winner of CGC's Genealogy Columnist Award of Excellence in two categories, in 1989. (11) Member of CGC.

There has *never* been a genealogy column in East Point.

GRADY COUNTY

At one time, GENEALOGY, ANYONE? by Floreda Duke Varick and Phyllis Rose Smith appeared in the *Cairo Messenger*, POB 30, Cairo, GA 31728, and covered research in Georgia and Florida. No other information was available.

HABERSHAM COUNTY: See De Lay's column under Fulton Co., GA.

HALL COUNTY:

The questionnaire was not returned, but the following information was given in the fifth edition of NGCD:

(1) HISTORY AND HERITAGE by Mrs. Sybil McRay, *Daily Times*, 345 Green St., NW, Gainesville, GA 30501. (2) Northeast Georgia. (3) *Daily Times*, Gainesville, GA 30501. (4) Weekly, usually in the Sunday edition. Occasionally, for lack of space, the column appears during one of the weekly editions. Two columns a month are devoted to genealogical queries and answers from readers over the United States. The other two columns are about history of northeast Georgia and write-ups on early families of the area. Mrs. McRay has printed inquiries from as far away as the British Isles. (5) About 1967. (6) Short queries are preferred. (7) Free. (8) Back columns available at the local library; some are on microfilm. (9) Mrs. McRay has several publications on Hall County, i.e., marriages, wills, cemetery records. Prices, list of publications, and details upon request.

HARRIS COUNTY: See Troup Co., GA.

HART COUNTY:

(1) PIONEERS OF HART COUNTY, GEORGIA, by Travis Parker, 2052 McLendon Ave., N.E., Atlanta, GA 30307-1807. (2) Hart Co., GA. (3) *The Hartwell Sun.* (4) Weekly. (5) July, 1978. (6) Query should relate to history of any family in Hart County. (7) Free. (8) Back columns have been edited and expanded, with an index, and are available from the author at the above address. Volume I is $21.00 postpaid, 200 pp., with separate indexes to 86 family histories and sources of information. Volume II, published in 1988, includes histories on approximately 100 additional families. (9) BIBLIOGRAPHY OF HART CO., GA, RESOURCE MATERIALS, $2.50 postpaid; MORTALITY SCHEDULES - 1850 FRANKLIN CO., GA, 1850 ELBERT CO., GA, 1860-1880 HART CO., GA, $2.50 postpaid; 1870 U.S. CENSUS HART CO., GA, (indexed) $6.50 postpaid; 1880 U.S. CENSUS HART CO., GA (indexed), $16.00 postpaid; HISTORY OF HART CO., GA, CHURCHES, $2.50 postpaid; HISTORY OF THE SHOAL CREEK BAPTIST CHURCH, HART CO., GA, 1789-1901, $5.00 postpaid; HISTORY OF THE SHOAL CREEK ACADEMY, HART CO., GA, $2.50 postpaid; HISTORICAL RESOURCES OF REED CREEK AND SHOAL CREEK DISTRICTS, HART CO., GA, $5.00 postpaid.

HEARD COUNTY: See Troup Co., GA.

HENRY COUNTY

Joel Dixon Wells does not publish a column in McDonough's *Henry and Clayton Sun.*

JACKSON COUNTY: See De Lay's column under Fulton Co., GA.

JASPER COUNTY

At one time, John Harvey was reportedly writing a column for the *Monticello News,* Monticello, GA 31064, but his questionnaire was never returned and no further information was available.

JEFFERSON COUNTY

(1) ANCESTORING by Jeanne and C.W. Stephens, POB 615, Wrens, GA 30833. (2) Jefferson, Burke, Richmond, Warren, Columbia, Washington, and other counties in Georgia. (3) *The Jefferson Reporter,* POB 277, Wrens, GA 30833. (4) Weekly. (5) 1979. (6) Requirements for a query: Who. Where. When. (7) Free. (8) First 79 columns are in book form, and a second book may also be available. Contact the writers at the address given in (l). (9) EARLY MARRIAGES, JEFFERSON CO., GA, 1805-1885, $5.00 from the columnists, includes postage and handling.

JENKINS COUNTY: See Screven Co., GA.

LOWNDES COUNTY

Lillian McRee reports she no longer writes a genealogy column in Valdosta, and that columns were not compiled and indexed. No other information was available.

MADISON COUNTY: See De Lay's column under Fulton Co., GA.

McDUFFIE COUNTY: See Columbia Co., GA.

MERIWETHER COUNTY: See Troup Co., GA.

MITCHELL COUNTY: See Clayton Co., GA.

PIKE COUNTY: See Clayton Co., GA.

RICHMOND COUNTY: See Jefferson Co., GA.

SCREVEN COUNTY

The questionnaire to Dixon Hollingsworth, POB 10, Sylvania, GA 30467, was not returned. The fifth edition of NGCD showed that his monthly column, GET ACQUAINTED WITH YOUR ANCESTORS, appeared from 1987 in *The Sylvania Telephone*. Columns were not compiled and indexed. The column covered Screven, Bulloch, Burke, Effingham, and Jenkins counties. The columnist also offered HISTORY OF SCREVEN COUNTY, with genealogy, about 500 pp., $62.50 plus $3.50 shipping.

SUMTER COUNTY

The *Americus Times-Recorder* apparently carries no genealogy column.

THOMAS COUNTY

Annette J. Stewart's questionnaire was not returned. Her twice-monthly column, GENEALOGY TODAY, appeared in the *Thomasville Times-Enterprise* from 1988 and covered research in southern Georgia, northern Florida, and southeast Alabama. Back columns were indexed and on file at Thomasville Cultural Center Library, POB 1597, Thomasville, GA 31792. Annette J. Stewart also offered some publications for sale and was a member of CGC. Her address: 401 Tuxedo Dr., Thomasville, GA 31792.

TROUP COUNTY

Shirley W. Bowen's HISTORY AND YOUR FAMILY is no longer being published. Her weekly column appeared for about ten years from 11 July 1979, in the *LaGrange Daily News*, LaGrange, GA 30241. The column covered Troup, Harris, Heard, and Meriwether counties in Georgia, and Randolph and Chambers counties in Alabama. Columns from 1979 to 1981 were published in two volumes, now out of print. At one time, indexing of the columns was in progress. The columnist also offered some Troup County publications for sale. Contact her about the availability of these publications at POB 2291, LaGrange, GA 30241.

WALKER COUNTY: See Catoosa Co., GA.

WALTON COUNTY: See De Lay's column under Fulton Co., GA.

WARREN COUNTY: See Jefferson Co., GA.

WASHINGTON COUNTY: See Jefferson Co., GA.

WILKES COUNTY: See Dougherty Co., GA.

HAWAII

HONOLULU COUNTY

There is *absolutely* no column called FAMILY TREE TALK in Laie. Any mail sent to FAMILY TREE TALK, 55-550 Nantida Loop #Q 275, Laie, HI 96762-1264 will be refused.

IDAHO

GENERAL: See Spokane Co., WA.

Juvanne Clezie's column, TRACING YOUR FAMILY ROOTS, was discontinued about 1979. It appeared in the *Idaho State Journal*, Pocatello, ID 83201. The Pocatello Public Library, 812 E. Clark St., Pocatello, ID 83201 may have back issues of the column.

ADA COUNTY

There is no longer a genealogy column published in the *Boise Statesman*. No other information was available.

BONNEVILLE COUNTY

The questionnaire to La Viece Smallwood, *Idaho Post Register*, 333 Northgate Mile, POB 1800, Idaho Falls, ID 83403, was not returned. OUT ON A LIMB appeared from 1984, and columns were not compiled or indexed.

TETON COUNTY

There is no genealogy column in Diggs.

ILLINOIS

GENERAL

The questionnaire to Carol Sims Rademacher was not returned. The following information appeared in the fifth edition of NGCD:

(1) CLIMBING THE GENEALOGICAL TREE with Carol Sims Rademacher, 705 Cathy Lane, Mt. Prospect, IL 60056. (2) Must have Illinois connection. (3) *Illinois Magazine*. Circulation area - nationwide. (4) 6 times yearly. (5) November, 1975. (6) Queries must have an Illinois connection; 50 words or less; a name, date, and locality. Include SASE for each query. Each query must be on a separate page, with submitter's name and address on each page. Columnist sometimes receives as many as ten queries typed on two or three pages with only one address, at the bottom of the last page. Columnist will not fill a whole column with one person's queries. (7) Free. (8) Queries are indexed in December issue and are in Illinois libraries.

The questionnaire to Sharon L. Todd was not returned. The following information appeared in the fifth edition of NGCD:

(1) ILLINOIS FAMILY HERITAGE by Sharon L. Todd, Rt. 1, Box 192, Monmouth, IL 61462. (2) Statewide. (3) Column appears in *American Genealogy Magazine*, POB 1587, Stephenville, TX 76401. Phone: (817) 965-6979. 1990 subscription rates: $12.00, 1 year; $21.00, 2 years. Single issue, $3.00. (4) Quarterly. (5) January, 1989. (6) Queries limited to about 50 words, and should concentrate on pre-1900 Illinois residents. All queries are published as space permits. Enclose SASE. (7) Free to both subscribers and non-subscribers. (8) Back columns are compiled and indexed for reader reference. (9) THE 1860 CENSUS OF MASON COUNTY, IL, $26.00 postpaid, 362 pp., 1988. Order from *American Genealogy Magazine*, at above address.

EASTERN ILLINOIS: See Vermilion Co., IL.

SOUTHEASTERN ILLINOIS: See Vanderburgh Co., IN.

CLARK COUNTY: See Vigo Co., IN.

There is no genealogy column in Marshall.

COOK COUNTY

United Methodists Today is no longer being published. No other information was available.

CRAWFORD COUNTY: See Vigo Co., IN.

CUMBERLAND COUNTY

Mary Holt, writer of IS YOUR NAME HERE? passed away August, 1982. The column covered the counties of Shelby, Effingham, Clark, Coles, Cumberland, and Jasper. No other information was available.

DeWITT COUNTY

KINFOLK KORNER by Fern L. Briggs and Phyllis Lynch is no longer being published, but the following information is given here because the columns were reprinted in book form:

(1) KINFOLK KORNER by Fern L. Briggs, 417 N. George St., Clinton, IL 61727-1515. (2) DeWitt, Macon, McLean, Piatt counties. (3) *Clinton Journal, Farmer City Journal, Decatur Herald* (Focus Section) in DeWitt, Piatt, and Logan counties, and *The Collector*, an antique paper, published monthly, queries only. (4) Weekly. (5) 1974-1976 by Phyllis Lynch; 12 August 1976 to 1 September 1987 by Fern L. Briggs. Fern Lane Briggs' columns are indexed and bound in two volumes and housed at the Warner Library, 120 W. Johnson St., Clinton, IL 61727, and at Farmer City Public Library, 109 E. Green St., Farmer City, IL 61842. Phyllis Lynch's columns are bound in one volume and housed at the Warner Library.

EDGAR COUNTY: See Vigo Co. IN.

MACON COUNTY: See DeWitt Co., IL.

MARION COUNTY: There are no genealogy columns in Patoka and Sandoval.

McLEAN COUNTY: See DeWitt Co., IL.

There is no genealogy column in Lexington.

PIATT COUNTY: See DeWitt Co., IL.

RICHLAND COUNTY

Barbara J. Craddock no longer writes RICHLAND ROUTES for the *Daily Mail*, Olney, IL 62450. The Olney Library, 401 E. Main St., may have a file of the column, which appeared about twice a month. No other information was available.

SANGAMON COUNTY

Wesley Johnston's FINDING YOUR OWN ROOTS is no longer published in *Illinois Times*. No other information was available.

TAZEWELL COUNTY

THE FOLK FINDER is no longer being published. However, the Tazewell County Genealogical Society, POB 312, Pekin, IL 61554-0312, lists queries free of charge in its *Tazewell Genealogical Monthly*, if the queries are about the Tazewell County area. THE FOLK FINDER queries, published in the *Pekin Daily Times* from about 1979, were also published in that periodical. All such queries may be accessed through the yearly index. The Society has copies with indexes of that monthly publication from the beginning (early 1970's) to date, as do other libraries in the county.

VERMILION COUNTY

(1) ILLIANA ANCESTORS by Joan Feistel Griffis, 105 Poland Road, Danville, IL 61832. (2) Paper has wide circulation in eastern Illinois and western Indiana. (3) *Commercial News*, Danville, IL 61832. (4) Weekly, on Sunday. (5) 1975. (6) Columnist will edit queries, if necessary. Please write surnames carefully in block letters and underline. (7) Free. (8) 1975 through 1982 have been indexed for the columnist's use, and she will check that index for SASE. The Danville Public Library, as well as other libraries, has microfilmed copies of the *Commercial News*. (9) ILLIANA ANCESTORS, Volume III: 1987, 1988, 1989, genealogy columns of the *Commercial News* by Joan Griffis, 8½" x 11", softbound, 105 pp., indexed, $10.00 postpaid. Index includes all surnames mentioned in the columns; ILLIANA ANCESTORS, Volume IV: 1990, 1991, 1992, 110 pp., surnames indexed (over 4,400 entries), $11.00 postpaid. Illinois residents add 7% sales tax to all book orders. Volumes include genealogical information helpful to researchers as well as queries. Order from the author at the above address. Volumes I and II, which covered 1981 - 1983 and 1984 - 1986, are apparently out of print. The Illiana Genealogical and Historical Society, POB 207, Danville, IL 61834, has several items for sale. Send SASE for list. Membership, $15.00 per year. (10) Column was rated number 2 of Indiana Genealogy Columns (out of 16), in Council of Genealogy Columnists contest. Illiana Genealogical and Historical Society no longer houses its collection at the Danville Public Library. Temporary home at 19 E. North St., Danville, IL 61832. Hours: 10:00 a.m. - 4:00 p.m., Wed. - Sat.; 5:00 - 8:00 p.m., Tues. Phone: 431-TREE. (11) Member of CGC.

WHITESIDE COUNTY

Jeannette Erickson's ASKING ABOUT ANCESTORS no longer appears in Sterling's *Daily Gazette*. The monthly column appeared from March, 1980 and printed queries about Whiteside County as well as those about Illinois in general. The newspapers are at the Sterling Library.

INDIANA

GENERAL: See Vicktoria Hizer's column under Marion Co., IN & Hancock Co., KY.

(1) WHO'S WHO, % *Electric Consumer*, POB 24517, Indianapolis, IN 46224. (2) All of Indiana. (3) *Electric Consumer*. (4) Occasional. (6) Queries should be typed or clearly written, and must include the writer's address. (7) Free. (8) Columns not compiled and indexed for reader reference.

NORTHERN INDIANA: See Saint Joseph Co., IN.

SOUTHEASTERN INDIANA: See Dearborn Co., IN.

SOUTHWESTERN INDIANA: See Martin Co., IN, Monroe Co., IN, & Vanderburgh Co., IN.

WESTERN INDIANA: See Vermilion Co., IL.

ALLEN COUNTY

Curt Witcher's column in the Fort Wayne *News Sentinel* was discontinued by the newspaper. No queries were accepted. The column began in early 1991 and stopped October, 1992. Curt Witcher's address: % Allen Co. Public Library, POB 2770, Ft. Wayne, IN 46802-2270. No other information was available.

The Fort Wayne *Journal-Gazette* does not run a genealogy column.

Melinda Newhard's column for the Fort Wayne *Tri-State Ancestry* was terminated March, 1978. The weekly column covered ancestral research in north Indiana, Ohio, and south Michigan. No other information was available.

BARTHOLOMEW COUNTY : See Jennings Co., IN, Monroe Co., IN, & Virgil B. Long's column under Jackson Co., IN.

FAMILY TREE is no longer published by the *Columbus Republic*. The Bartholomew County Library, 5th & Lafayette Sts., Columbus, IN 47201, may have a file of the column. No other information was available.

BROWN COUNTY: See Monroe Co., IN &Virgil B. Long's column under Jackson Co., IN.

CLARK COUNTY: See Floyd Co., IN, Jefferson Co., IN, & Scott Co., IN.

KNOW YOUR KIN by Sandra Brown is no longer published by the *Charlestown Courier*. No other information was available.

CLAY COUNTY: See Putnam Co., IN & Vigo Co., IN.

The questionnaire to Ben Coffman, POB 67, Centerpoint, IN 47840 was not returned. His column was reportedly published during 1992 and 1993 in *Brazil Times* and *Clay City News*.

CRAWFORD COUNTY: See Floyd Co., IN.

DAVIESS COUNTY: See Martin Co., IN & Monroe Co., IN.

DEARBORN COUNTY: See Jefferson Co., IN.

Chris McHenry's CLIMBING THE FAMILY TREE is no longer published in *Dearborn County Register* and *Rising Sun Recorder*, Register Publications, POB 328, Lawrenceburg, IN 47025. It appeared weekly in each paper, from 1975. Column covered southeast Indiana: Dearborn, Ohio, Switzerland, Ripley, and Franklin counties. Columns were not compiled or indexed, but bound copies of the newspapers are at the local library. Queries sent to the newspaper are forwarded to Dearborn County Library where they and Historical Society try to provide answers.

DECATUR COUNTY: See Jennings Co., IN.

DeKALB COUNTY: See Williams Co., OH.

ELKHART COUNTY

There are no genealogy columns in Elkhart or New Paris.

FLOYD COUNTY

(1) FAMILY BRANCHES by Vicky Zuverink, 3834 Dogwood Rd., Floyds Knobs, IN 47119-9359. (2) Clark, Crawford, Floyd, Harrison, Jefferson, Orange, Perry, Scott, and Washington counties. (3) *The Tribune*, New Albany, IN. (4) Weekly, on Tuesday. (5) 23 June 1991. (6) Queries must have a date to establish a time period, and a connection to the above-named counties. Include SASE for all correspondence. (7) Free. (8) Clipped, indexed and will be on microfilm at New Albany-Floyd County Public Library. (10) Columnist will print information concerning research facilities, family reunions, research tips, new books, and genealogical meetings. (11) Member of CGC.

FRANKLIN COUNTY: See Dearborn Co., IN.

GREENE COUNTY: See Monroe Co., IN & Vigo Co., IN.

HANCOCK COUNTY

Lynn German's SUGAR CREEK ANCESTORS, which began in October, 1983, no longer appears in *The New Palestine Press*. The monthly column ran queries on Hancock and Shelby counties. The local libraries may carry copies.

HARRISON COUNTY: See Floyd Co., IN.

HENDRICKS COUNTY: See Putnam Co., IN.

HENRY COUNTY: See Wayne Co., IN.

HOWARD COUNTY

Judy Lausch's monthly column no longer appears in the *Kokomo Tribune*. It began about 1987, ended in summer, 1994, and covered research in Howard County and the surrounding area. Queries were placed in a surname file maintained at the Kokomo-Howard County Public Library. In answer to requests, approximate date of publication and query number was sent, if SASE included with query. This service may still be available.

JACKSON COUNTY: See Jennings Co., IN, Monroe Co., IN, & Scott Co., IN.

Jonette K. Johnson's JACKSON COUNTY ANCESTORS is no longer carried in *The Brownstone Banner* or Seymour newspapers. It appeared twice monthly from November, 1982 until October, 1992 and covered Jackson County research. The newspaper is on microfilm at Seymour Public Library, Seymour, IN 47274. That library also may have an 1886 history of Jackson County for sale.

There is no genealogy column in the Crothersville *Austin-Crothersville News*.

(1) Genealogy column by Virgil B. Long, 637 North Poplar St., Seymour, IN 47274. (2) Bartholomew, Brown, Jackson, Jefferson, Jennings, Lawrence, Monroe, Scott, and Washington counties. (3) *The Seymour Daily Tribune*. (4) Every other Friday. (5) October, 1994. (7) Free to anyone researching in any of the above-mentioned counties. (8) Columns have not been compiled or indexed but are available at the Seymour Public Library, Seymour, IN 47274.

JEFFERSON COUNTY: See Floyd Co., IN, Jennings Co., IN, Scott Co., IN, & Virgil B. Long's column under Jackson Co., IN.

George Miller plans to retire from writing his column sometime in 1995. The information given below was listed in the fifth edition of NGCD:

(1) FAMILY TREES, TWIGS AND CHIPS by Al and Margaret Spiry, 2729 Arbor Avenue, Cincinnati, OH 45209-2206. (2) Indiana counties of Clark, Dearborn, Jefferson, Jennings, Ohio, Ripley, Scott, and Switzerland. Kentucky counties of

Boone, Carroll, Gallatin, Grant, Henry, Oldham, Owen, Shelby, and Trimble. (3) *The Madison Courier* and *The Weekly Herald*, 310 Courier Square, Madison, IN 47250. (4) Each Tuesday in *The Madison Courier* and each Friday in *The Weekly Herald*. (5) A feature column, IT REMINDS ME, started carrying genealogical material in 1964. The FAMILY TREES, TWIGS AND CHIPS column started 4 December 1971, totally devoted to genealogy. George H. Miller wrote the column from 1964 to 1995. The Spirys took over October 10, 1995. (6) Queries must have a name and date and some location in one of the above named counties of the newspaper's reading area. If queries are handwritten, please print the names. Those submitting queries should enclose SASE, if they wish to have an estimated date of publication. Queries are usually printed two or three weeks after they are received. (7) Free. (8) Back copies are available on microfilm and in a clipping file at the Madison-Jefferson County Public Library, 4520 W. Main St., Madison, IN 47250. Some clippings go in files of major pioneer families. Columns are not indexed. (9) The newspapers charge $1.25 a copy by mail. The Public Library (address above) will photocopy a column for $1.00 plus SASE, if column is available in clipping file. The most economical way to get all weekly columns is to subscribe to *The Weekly Herald*, at the address given in (3). Current subscription rates for *The Madison Courier* are $82.00 a year in Indiana and Kentucky, six months for $43.00 - $88.00 a year for all other mainland states, six months for $46.00. Current subscription rates for *The Weekly Herald* are $17.25 a year in Indiana and Kentucky, and $21.75 a year for all other mainland states. Write for rates for Hawaii and Alaska and foreign countries. (10) The column carries an average of 390 to 410 queries a year, and during the life of the column queries have been received from all states plus several foreign countries. Besides the queries, the column carries general advice on researching family information in the counties noted, with the greatest emphasis on Jefferson and Switzerland counties in Indiana, and Carroll and Trimble counties in Kentucky.

JENNINGS COUNTY: See Scott Co., IN, Jefferson Co., IN, &Virgil B. Long's column under Jackson Co., IN.

(1) BRANCHES OF THE WINDING WATERS by Lilian H. Carmer, 3345 South CR 800E, Dupont, IN 47231. (2) Jennings and surrounding counties of Bartholomew, Decatur, Jackson, Jefferson, Ripley, and Scott counties. (3) *North Vernon Plain Dealer*, North Vernon, IN 47265. (4) Monthly. (5) March, 1983. (6) Queries must have connection to the above named counties. (7) Free. (8) Columns have been compiled and indexed and are available to the public at the Jennings County Public Library, North Vernon, or the Jennings County Recorder's Office, Vernon. (9) Subscription to *The North Vernon Plain Dealer* and *North Vernon Sun* is $21.00 in counties listed, $25.50 elsewhere in Indiana and in surrounding states, $29.00 elsewhere. (10) Jennings County was founded in 1817 following Indiana's admission to the Union in 1816. Vernon is the county seat, and the entire town, including the cemetery, is listed on the National Register. John Vawter was Vernon's founder. Lilian H. Carmer is Vice-President of the Indiana Genealogical Society and a member of the Jennings County and Bartholomew County

Genealogical societies, Jennings County Historical Society, and Jennings County Preservation Association. (11) Member of CGC since 1988.

KNOX COUNTY: See Monroe Co., IN.

KOSCIUSKO COUNTY

(1) RELATIVELY SPEAKING by Doris McManis Camden, POB 214, Warsaw, IN 46581-0214. (2) Kosciusko and Noble counties. (3) *Mail-Journal* and *The Paper*. (4) Twice monthly. (5) October, 1980. (6) Must pertain to Kosciusko or Noble counties, be concise, 50-word limit; typed or printed. (7) Free. (8) Some columns are at Kosciusko County Historical Society, Genealogy Section Library, Old Jail Museum, Indiana and Main Sts., Warsaw, IN 46580. Open Thurs. - Sun., 1:00 to 4:00 p.m., except possibly holiday weekends. (9) Kosciusko County Historical Society, Genealogy Section, POB 1071, Warsaw, IN 46581, publishes a quarterly, *Our Missing Links*, $10.00 a year, 24 pp. each issue. There is also a free column in this quarterly written by Doris Camden. Call (219) 267-1078 for confirmation of hours. (11) Member of CGC.

LAKE COUNTY

Apparently Archibald McKinlay does not write a column called CALUMET ROOTS for the *Hammond Times*.

LAWRENCE COUNTY: See Monroe Co., IN &Virgil B. Long's column under Jackson Co., IN.

MARION COUNTY

ANCESTORITIS by Willard Heiss, which appeared weekly in the Indianapolis News from 1977, ceased publication at the time of Mr. Heiss' retirement on 27 November 1986. Columns are at the Indiana State Library. Mr. Heiss passed away in 1988.

(1) INDIANA ANCESTORS by Vicktoria Hizer, *The Indianapolis Star*, POB 145, Indianapolis, IN 46206. (2) Indiana. (3) *The Indianapolis Star*. (4) Weekly, on Sunday. (5) The column started in 1963 as HOOSIER ANCESTORS. Vicktoria Hizer took over September, 1977. (6) Query must mention Indiana and should be limited to 50 words, plus dates and sender's name and address. One query per letter preferred, clearly stated, with typed or printed surnames to minimize errors. Query number and approximate date of publication sent if SASE accompanies request. (7) Free. (8) Indexes and columns are in the State Library from June, 1963 through 29 June 1975. The Allen County Public Library, 900 Webster St., Ft. Wayne, IN 46802, indexed the column for many years but stopped after 1984. The Library has the index for 1973-1984.

MARTIN COUNTY: See Monroe Co., IN.

Robert Conalty-Webber's weekly column, YOUR FAMILY HISTORY, is no longer published in Martin County's *Loogootee Tribune* (from May, 1988) and Daviess County's *Tri-County News* (from September, 1988). The column covered research in southwest Indiana and Daviess, Martin, and Pike counties. The columns are available at the Indiana State Library, Genealogy Division; and at the Loogootee Public Library.

MONROE COUNTY: See Virgil B. Long's column under Jackson Co., IN.

(1) FAMILY TREE LEAVES by Mrs. Mona D. Robinson, 1717 East Hunter Ave., Bloomington, IN 47401. (2) Indiana counties of Monroe, Lawrence, Greene, Brown, Owen, Morgan, Orange, Martin, Jackson, Bartholomew, Washington, Daviess, Knox, and Vanderburgh. Mrs. Robinson will run queries for the southwest corner of the state, but readership does not reach that far. (3) *Sunday Herald Times*, %Life Style Department, 1900 S. Walnut St., Bloomington, IN 47401. (4) Weekly, on Sunday. (5) December, 1974. (6) 35 words or less, excluding name, address, and dates. More than one query may be sent in an envelope, but one subject to a query, please. (7) Free. (8) Columns not compiled. Surname indexes available from author. Indexes are available for each year since 1975, at $2.50 per year, including postage and handling. (Specify year desired.) Back columns available at the Monroe County Public Library, Monroe County Genealogical Society Library, and the Allen County Public Library, 900 Webster St., Ft. Wayne, IN 46802. (9) Mona Robinson's book on Indiana genealogy, WHO'S YOUR HOOSIER ANCESTOR? was published in summer, 1992, by Indiana University Press. The book is available from the author or from Indiana University Press; in soft-cover, $12.95; hardback, $27.95; add $3.00 for postage and handling. (11) Member of CGC.

MONTGOMERY COUNTY: See Putnam Co., IN.

(1) FAMILY ROOTS by Karen Zach, RR 7, POB 43, Crawfordsville, IN 47933. (2) Montgomery County and surrounding area. (3) *Montgomery, Your County Magazine*. (4) Monthly. (5) 1976. (6) 50 words or less. (7) Free. (8) Columns are at the local library. (11) Member of CGC.

MORGAN COUNTY: See Monroe Co., IN & Putnam Co., IN.

The following column succeeded BECKY'S BIT, which started about 1963 in the *Times* and 1967 in the *Reporter*.

(1) MORGAN COUNTY YESTERDAY by Dale Drake, 1195 Robb Hill Rd., Martinsville, IN 46151. (2) Morgan County and surrounding counties. (3) *Mooresville Times*, 23 E. Main St., Mooresville, IN 46158; *Martinsville Daily Reporter*, 60 S. Jefferson St., Martinsville, IN 46151. (4) Bi-weekly. (5) April, 1993. (6) Morgan County connection. (7) Free. (8) Columns not compiled and indexed, but back issues of the paper are available from the columnist for cost of

copies and postage. (9) MORGAN COUNTY SCRAPBOOK II, 510 pp., $27.50 + $4.00 postage and handling. Book contains information on Morgan County churches and schools. (10) Columnist is Morgan County historian and also a professional genealogist. Send SASE for brochure. (11) Member of CGC.

Judge Nobel K. Littel does not write a genealogy column in Morgan County.

NOBLE COUNTY: See Kosciusko Co., IN.

The *Noble County American*, in Albion, is no longer being published. It was said to carry Robert C. Gagen's SPEAKING OF GENEALOGY. No other information was available.

OHIO COUNTY: See Dearborn Co., IN & Jefferson Co., IN.

ORANGE COUNTY: See Floyd Co., IN & Monroe Co., IN.

OWEN COUNTY: See Monroe Co., IN, Putnam Co., IN, & Vigo Co., IN.

Dixie Kline's column, OWEN COUNTY ANCESTORS, which ran from 1971 on an irregular basis, ceased publication in 1987, when the columnist married and moved from Spencer. There is no column at present, and the local newspaper no longer accepts queries, but *may* print queries as letters to the editor. There is much local genealogy at the Spencer-Owen County Public Library.

PARKE COUNTY: See Putnam Co., IN & Vigo Co., IN.

PERRY COUNTY: See Floyd Co., IN & Spencer Co., IN (9).

Agnes Sutton's TALES OF OUR PAST has not been published for many years. It appeared in Tobinsport's *Cannelton News*. No other information was available.

PIKE COUNTY: See Martin Co., IN.

PULASKI COUNTY: Mrs. Oral Burgess' KOUNTRY KIN is no longer published. Columns were microfilmed and are available in the Genealogical Library, Salt Lake City, UT.

PUTNAM COUNTY: See Putnam Co., IN & Vigo Co., IN.

Nancy Clifford's HERITAGE TRAIL no longer appears in Greencastle's *Banner-Graphic*. The column appeared about twice monthly from 25 November 1979 until 23 November 1982 and carried queries about Clay, Hendricks, Montgomery, Morgan, Owen, Parke, and Putnam counties. Columns were not indexed, but should be available at Putnam County Library, Greencastle, IN 46135 and at DePauw Archives, in Roy 0. West Library, DePauw University, Greencastle, IN 46135.

RIPLEY COUNTY: See Dearborn Co., IN, Jefferson Co., IN, & Jennings Co., IN.

Rowena Mathews' column, GENEALOGY, was published in the *Versailles Republican* during the 1970's. She died in 1981. Her columns have not been indexed, but are at the Carnegie Library, Osgood, IN 47037.

SAINT JOSEPH COUNTY

(1) MICHIANA ROOTS by Carol Collins, *South Bend Tribune*, 225 W. Colfax, South Bend, IN 46626. (2) Northern Indiana and southern Michigan. (3) *South Bend Tribune*. (4) Weekly, on Sunday. (5) 1972. (6) Query should pertain to interest area and should be concise, preferably typed. Surnames, at least, should be printed. Letter may contain more than one query per sheet of paper, if each query is numbered. (7) Free. (8) Column's first four years are in book form, $15.75 postpaid from Carol Collins, at the address given in (1). Ft. Wayne Library, Ft. Wayne, IN has a complete set of the columns, as do the State Library and South Bend Library. (9) MICHIANA ROOTS, Volume I, $15.75, covers 1972-1977; Volume II, 1977-1980, is out of print. (11) Member of CGC.

SCOTT COUNTY: See Floyd Co., IN, Jefferson Co., IN, Jennings Co., IN, & Virgil B. Long's column under Jackson Co., IN.

(1) SCOTT COUNTY ANCESTORS by Mrs. Jeannie Noe Carlisle, POB 268, Lexington, IN 47138-0268. (2) Indiana counties of Clark, Jackson, Jefferson, Jennings, Scott, and Washington. (3) *Scott County Journal and Chronicle*. (4) Every 4 to 6 weeks. (5) About 1970. (6) 50 words or less. Prefer a connection to area, but will place any query in column. (7) Free. (8) There are plans for an index. (9) LEXINGTON, A PIONEER TOWN, 95 pp., $7.00; THE EARLY HISTORY OF SCOTT CO., IN, 1820-1 870, 32 pp., $5.00; SCOTTSBURG CEMETERY RECORD, 1986, plus 1989 additions and corrections, 219 pp., $24.00; LEXINGTON TWP. CEMETERY BOOK, 1813-1988, 140 pp., $17.00; HISTORY OF LEOTA AND SURROUNDING FINLEY TWP., 22 pp, $5.00; SCOTT COUNTY CEMETERY BOOK, VIENNA TWP., 124 pp., $14.00; SCHOOLS, LEXINGTON TWP., 1817-1929, $8.00. Write for details. (10) Send SASE for flyer of items available in Scott County. *Lexington Historical Society, Inc. Newsletter* is $5.00 per year; *Scott County Genealogical Society Newsletter*, dues $10.00 annually. Sample of both newsletters for SASE with two stamps. Free queries in both newsletters. Lexington Historical Society is surnames only.

SHELBY COUNTY: See Hancock Co., IN.

SPENCER COUNTY

(1) HOOSIER ANCESTORS by Becky Middleton, %Spencer County Historical Society, 210 Walnut St., Rockport, IN 47635-1398. (2) Spencer County and surrounding area. (3) *Rockport Journal Democrat*. (4) Weekly. (5) 1986. (6) Query

should contain as much information as possible about the person or persons being researched. (7) Free. (8) The first six years of HOOSIER ANCESTORS (1986-1991) have been indexed, 310 pp. Available from the Spencer County Historical Society, $25.00. 1992 and 1993 may also be indexed. (9) SPENCER COUNTY CEMETERY INSCRIPTIONS, Vols. I-III, $37.00 each, indexed; HISTORY OF WARRICK, SPENCER AND PERRY COUNTIES, IN, 837 pp. plus index for each county, a reprint of the 1885 Goodspeed, $50.00; 1879 ILLUSTRATED ATLAS, SPENCER COUNTY, $22.00, indexed; 1968 ROCKPORT SESQUICENTENNIAL, $6.00; MINUTE BOOK, LITTLE PIGEON CREEK BAPTIST CHURCH, 1816-1840, $11.00; LINCOLN AND HIS NEIGHBORS, $4.50; THE MISSING CHAPTER IN THE LIFE OF ABRAHAM LINCOLN, $17.00. (10) Research will be done by Society members in census, newspapers, and cemeteries for $5.00 an hour, plus copies. Queries are accepted for weekly column or quarterly newsletter free of charge.

STEUBEN COUNTY: See Williams Co., OH.

SULLIVAN COUNTY: See Vigo Co., IN.

There is no longer a genealogy column in *The Sullivan Union*. The Vincennes and Knox County Public Library, 502 N. 7th St., Vincennes, IN 47591, may have copies of this column. No other information was available.

SWITZERLAND COUNTY: See Dearborn Co., IN & Jefferson Co., IN.

TIPTON COUNTY

(1) GENERATIONS by Donna Ekstrom, %Tipton Library, 127 E. Madison, Tipton, IN 46072. (2) Tipton County. (3) *Tipton County Tribune*. (4) The last Tuesday of each month. (5) January, 1988. (6) Query must pertain to Tipton County. (7) Free. (8) Columns not compiled, but they are accessible to the public at Tipton Library. (10) Column also reviews new books added to the library's genealogy collection. The columnist is a library employee and is in charge of the Genealogy/Local History Collection. (11) Member of CGC.

UNION COUNTY: See Wayne Co., IN.

VANDERBURGH COUNTY: See Monroe Co., IN.

Marjorie Blocher Kinsey's questionnaire was not returned, but at one time she wrote a bi-weekly column that appeared in the Sunday edition of *The Evansville Courier*, POB 286, Evansville, IN 47702. The column began 13 October 1991. The column covered research in southwestern Indiana, northwestern Kentucky, and southeastern Illinois.

VERMILLION COUNTY: See Vigo Co., IN.

VIGO COUNTY

(1) GENEALOGY by Linda Herrick Swisher, *Tribune-Star*, 721 Wabash Ave., POB 149, Terre Haute, IN 47808. (2) Indiana counties of Clay, Greene, Owen, Parke, Putnam, Sullivan, Vermillion, and Vigo; Illinois counties of Edgar, Crawford, and Clark. (3) *Tribune-Star*. (4) Weekly, on Sunday. (5) 22 January 1995. (6) None. Spell out -- do not abbreviate. Queries can pertain to any locale, but especially Indiana/Illinois. If SASE included, columnist will send photocopy of column in which query appears. (7) Free. (8) Columns not compiled and indexed, but are accessible at the local library. (10) Columnist does not do research for hire. She also writes a column for *Ancestry* magazine.

NOTE: This column replaces Dorothy J. Clark's column, which appeared each Sunday in the *Tribune-Star* from 1978 until her retirement in December, 1994. Dorothy J. Clark had a complete file of her columns, completely indexed and bound by year. Copies are at the Vigo County Library.

WARRICK COUNTY: See Spencer Co., IN (9).

WASHINGTON COUNTY: See Floyd Co., IN, Monroe Co., IN, Scott Co., IN, & Virgil B. Long's column under Jackson Co., IN.

There is no longer a column in Salem's *Washington Press*. The columnist, Helen Burgess, died in 1974. The Salem Library, POB 150, Salem, IN 47167, may have copies of the newspaper. No other information was available.

WAYNE COUNTY

(1) THE ECHO by Bob Hansen, 99 S. Perry St., Hagerstown, IN 47346-1521. (2) Parts of Henry, Wayne, and Union counties. (3) *Hagerstown Exponent*. (4) Occasional. (5) 1987. (6) Brevity preferred. (7) Free. (8) Columns have not been compiled and indexed, but the newspapers are available at the Hagerstown Library.

WHITE COUNTY

ANCESTORS by Merlin C. Finnell was discontinued March, 1980, by the *Journal and Courier*. It appeared on Sundays. Copies of all four years of the column's publication are available in both the Indiana State Library, Genealogy Division, Indianapolis, IN 46204, and the Ft. Wayne Library, Genealogy Division, Ft. Wayne, IN 46802.

WHITLEY COUNTY

Tri-County Truth, Churubusco, has *never* published a genealogy column.

IOWA

GENERAL: See Linn Co., IA & Holt Co., MO.

SOUTHWESTERN IOWA: See Page Co., IA & Union Co., IA.

WESTERN IOWA: See Washington Co., NE.

ADAIR COUNTY

Dorothy Mayes' column, ANQUESTERS, was discontinued about 1989. Queries were published in the *Adair County Free Press* about once a month and concerned Adair County and surrounding counties. Copies of the newspaper may be available at the Greenfield Public Library.

APPANOOSE COUNTY

Gladys Waite DePuy no longer writes her weekly column for the *Ad-Express/Iowegian*, Centerville, IA 52544. She retired and moved to Colorado. The column began in 1982, but no ending date was given. Columns not compiled or indexed. Microfilm copies of the newspaper are at Drake Public Library, Centerville, IA.

CLAYTON COUNTY

Mrs. Myra Voss of VOSS' GENIE did not return her questionnaire. Information from the fifth edition of NGCD is given here:

(1) VOSS' GENIE by Mrs. Myra Voss, Clayton County Genealogist/Historian, Elkader, IA 52043-0295. Phone: (319) 245-1418. (2) Clayton County. (3) *Clayton County Register*, Elkader, IA, in the Market Basket section, which is also enclosed with the *Monona Billboard*, Monona, IA (northern part of county), and is placed in rural mailboxes in the southeastern part of Clayton County, IA; so coverage is almost all of Clayton County, plus other subscribers. (4) Weekly. (5) July, 1983. (6) Relatives or ancestors who live in, or once lived in, Clayton County, IA. (7) Queries are usually $3.00; no charge for information for the general public. (8) Columns are in the process of being indexed. Upon completion, index will be on genealogical shelves at Elkader Public Library. (9) Contact the columnist for information about joining Clayton County Genealogical Society and about the Society's publications. (10) VOSS' GENIE is a public service column. (22) Member of CGC.

FRANKLIN COUNTY

A questionnaire to Judy Jeffrie Gallogly, 211 Oak Hill Dr., Hampton, IA 50441 was not returned. She reportedly wrote a monthly column that began in January, 1994.

GRUNDY COUNTY

There is no genealogy column in *The Collectors' News*, Grundy Center, IA.

HARRISON COUNTY: See Woodbury Co., IA.

KEOKUK COUNTY

There is no genealogy column in Sigourney.

LINN COUNTY

(1) DEAR GENIE, POB 175, Cedar Rapids, IA 52406. (2) Iowa connection. (3) *Cedar Rapids Gazette* (circulation over 90,000). (4) Weekly, on Sunday, when space is available. (5) January, 1973. (6) Queries have a 50 word limit and must be clearly typed or printed, with an Iowa connection. Name and address must be included. (7) Free. (8) Indexes to the columns are in the libraries at Des Moines, Iowa City, and at the Linn County Genealogical Research Center, 101 8th Ave., S.E., Cedar Rapids, IA 52401. Indexes cover 1973-1985. Linn County Genealogical Research Center is working on later years.

MARSHALL COUNTY

SEARCHING YESTERYEAR by Central Iowa Genealogical Society was discontinued by the *Marshalltown Times Republican*, when the paper changed hands. The column ran irregularly, about twice a month, from 9 March 1983. Final publication date was not given. *Times-Republican* is on microfilm and available to the public at the local library.

MILLS COUNTY

(1) LOOKING BACK (formerly BRANCHES AND TWIGS) by Beverly Boileau, RR1, Box 3, Henderson, IA 51541. (2) Mills County. (3) Glenwood *Opinion-Tribune*. (4) Weekly. (5) 2 June 1983. (7) Free. (8) Columns have been compiled and indexed by the columnist and individual columns are available from her at the address given in (1). Enclose SASE.

MONONA COUNTY: See Woodbury Co., IA.

MONROE COUNTY

There is no genealogy column in the Albia newspaper.

PAGE COUNTY

Betty Ankeny's PAGES FROM THE PAST is no longer published in the *Clarinda Herald-Journal*. The weekly column, which began in 1979, covered research in southwest Iowa, northwest Missouri, northeast Kansas, and southeast Nebraska. Columns were indexed. All issues and indexes are in the local library and museum library. Columnist will still do research, and will be happy to check column index. Contact her at 420 S. 16th, Clarinda, IA 51632. Include SASE.

PLYMOUTH COUNTY

There is no genealogy column in the *Le Mars Sentinel*.

POLK COUNTY

The Des Moines Sunday Register carries no genealogy column.

SCOTT COUNTY

There is no genealogy column in Davenport's *Quad-City Times*.

UNION COUNTY

The questionnaire to Union County Genealogical Society was not returned. Information from the fifth edition of NGCD is given below:

(1) TRACING YOUR ROOTS by Union County Genealogical Society, % Creston Public Library, 310 N. Maple, Creston, IA 50801. (2) Basically Union County, but paper goes to all southwestern Iowa counties and many other states. (3) *Creston News Advertiser*, POB 126, Creston, IA 50801. (4) About quarterly. More often, if more queries. Paper will print only about six at a time, and some are not submitted if columnist has answered them thoroughly. (5) About 1980. (6) Queries must be concise, clear, to the point, and no more than 50 words. (7) Free, both in paper and Society's newsletter. (8) All queries are published in the Society newsletters, which are at the local library, with indexes. Copies are at the home of the query coordinator, Irma M. Miller. Accessible to the public by a phone call. (9) GREENLAWN CEMETERY BOOK (Afton, IA), 1861 - 1987. 3500 burials, lot owners -- all indexed. $23.00 postpaid; TOMBSTONE INSCRIPTIONS OF JONES, UNION, HIGHLAND AND DOUGLAS TOWNSHIPS, contains all cemeteries in those townships, except Greenlawn, Graceland, and the Catholic cemeteries. Includes Maple Hill, at Cromwell. Every-name index, 112 pp., $12.00 postpaid; UNION COUNTY (IOWA) CEMETERIES, includes the three Catholic cemeteries in the county. Fully indexed, 144 pp., $12.00 postpaid. Society also has

copies, at $.50 each, of all obituaries of people buried in Graceland Cemetery (Creston, IA) from the mid-1930's and Calvary Catholic Cemetery since December, 1969. Also available, in 8 volumes, spiral bound, plus a separate volume with every-name index: all the genealogical/historical news from the original *Afton Enterprise*, from 1880-1893 (some missing issues). 125-140 pp. each, $12.50 each, postpaid. (10) Society membership is $5.00 per calendar year which includes the quarterly newsletter.

WOODBURY COUNTY

The questionnaire to Earl L. Belt was not returned. Information from the fifth edition of NGCD is given below:

(1) COLLECTING ANCESTORS by Earl L. Belt, 2657 S. Palmetto, Sioux City, IA 51106. (2) Harrison, Monona, and Woodbury counties, Iowa; Burt County, Nebraska. (3) The *Onawa Democrat*, 720 E. Iowa Ave., Onawa, IA 51040; The *Onawa Sentinel*, 1014 Ninth St., Onawa, IA 51040. (4) Monthly, in each paper. (5) December, 1983. See also (8). (6) Query must be in relation to counties named above. (7) Free. Copy not furnished to writer. (8) Copies are on file in the Onawa Public Library. Copies of the COLLECTING ANCESTORS column previously published in the *Sioux City Journal* (1978-1979) are available in the Sioux City Public Library. (10) Please send queries to the columnist at the address given, rather than to the papers.

KANSAS

GENERAL: See Holt Co., MO.

Merle Ganier no longer writes YOUR KANSAS FAMILY TREE for *Kanhistique*. The monthly column covered Kansas-related queries and ran from 1977. Columns for 1977-1980 were indexed and in book form. That book may still be available from Merle Ganier for $3.00. Copies of *Kanhistique* are probably on file at the Kansas Historical Society, Topeka, KS. Reportedly, Gayle W. Graham has taken over the column. Contact *Kanhistique* to see if the column was replaced: POB 7, Ellsworth, KS 67439.

EASTERN KANSAS : See Neosho Co., KS.

NORTH CENTRAL KANSAS: See Saline Co., KS

NORTHEASTERN KANSAS: See Page Co., IA.

MARION COUNTY

Mary Katherine Ford was unable to start a genealogy column, but at one time she was willing to check available sources to help researchers. Her address in the fifth edition of NGCD: 401 S. Cedar, Marion, KS 66861.

MORTON COUNTY: See Lubbock Co., TX.

NEOSHO COUNTY

(1) PAGES FROM THE PAST by Warren H. Fitch, 1016 W. First St., Chanute, KS 66720. (2) Eastern Kansas. (3) *Chanute Kansas Tribune* and *Southeast Kansas Good News*. (4) Monthly. (5) January, 1980. (6) Less than 60 words. Query must have an eastern Kansas connection. (7) Free. (8) Mr. Fitch has compiled back columns in a notebook.

SALINE COUNTY

The *Salina Journal* no longer carries Judy Lilly's SMOKY VALLEY ROOTS. The column, which started October, 1979, concerned north central Kansas, and was not compiled or indexed. Newspapers are on microfilm at the Salina Public Library.

SEWARD COUNTY

The questionnaire was not returned, but it is reported that Florence Palmer Herring has a column. Her address: POB 1448, Liberal, KS 67905-1448. No other information was available.

KENTUCKY

EASTERN KENTUCKY: See Lewis Co., KY (9) & Pike Co., KY.

NORTHWESTERN KENTUCKY: See Vanderburgh Co., IN.

ADAIR COUNTY

(1) BACKWARD GLANCES by Michael C. Watson, 204 High St., Columbia, KY 42728. (2) Adair, Casey, Cumberland, Green, Metcalfe, Russell and Taylor counties. (3) *Adair Progress*. (4) Weekly. (5) 1983. (6) Brevity; 50 words or less preferred. (7) Free. (8) Columns available at the local library. (9) Contact the columnist at the above address about numerous volumes he has for sale on Adair and surrounding counties.

BOONE COUNTY: See Jefferson Co., IN.

BOYD COUNTY: See Lewis Co., KY & Wayne Co., WV.

Evelyn Jackson's REFLECTIONS probably no longer appears in the *Ashland Daily Independent*. The Ashland Public Library, 1740 Central Ave., Ashland, KY 41101, may have copies of the column, which appeared on Mondays or Thursdays. No other information was available.

BREATHITT COUNTY

Pam Haddix' weekly column, LOOKING FOR LEADS, which began 31 October 1985, has not been published since 1989. It appeared in *Jackson Times* and printed queries and information about Breathitt, Owsley, Perry, and Wolfe counties. At one time, it was reported that the columns were compiled and indexed and were available from Breathitt County Genealogical Society, % Breathitt County Public Library, 1024 College Ave., Jackson, KY 41339. However, a notation from Breathitt County Genealogical Society states that the columns are not compiled and indexed and accessible to the public. No other information was available.

BRECKINRIDGE COUNTY: See Hancock Co., KY & final entry under Ohio Co., KY.

There is no genealogy column in Hardinsburg's *Herald News*.

CALLOWAY COUNTY: See Henry Co., TN.

CARROLL COUNTY: See Jefferson Co., IN.

CARTER COUNTY: See Lewis Co., KY.

CASEY COUNTY: See Adair Co., KY.

CUMBERLAND COUNTY: See Adair Co., KY.

DAVIESS COUNTY: See Hancock Co., KY & final entry under Ohio Co., KY.

FLEMING COUNTY: See Lewis Co., KY (9).

FULTON COUNTY

Eunice Mitchell's KENTUCKY KIN ran for about 10 years, terminating around 1979. Columns are at the library in Fulton, KY 42041. The column appeared weekly, on Fridays.

GALLATIN COUNTY: See Jefferson Co., IN.

GRANT COUNTY: See Jefferson Co., IN.

GRAVES COUNTY: See Henry Co., TN.

GRAYSON COUNTY: See Hancock Co., IN.

GREEN COUNTY: See Adair Co., KY.

GREENUP COUNTY: See Lewis Co., KY.

HANCOCK COUNTY

Mrs. Dorothy A. Watkins' questionnaire was not returned. Information from her listing in the fifth edition of NGCD is given below:

(1) CLIMB YOUR FAMILY TREE by Mrs. Dorothy A. Watkins, R 1, Box 950, Hawesville, KY 42348. (2) Kentucky counties of Breckinridge, Daviess, Grayson, Hancock, and Ohio; several states, including VA, NC, SC, TN, AR, and IN. (3) *Hancock County Clarion*, Hawesville, KY 42348. (4) Weekly. (5) October, 1986. (6) No limit. Query must be on ring note paper or typing paper. Columnist uses any information sent to her. (7) Free. (8) Back columns compiled and indexed. (9) Columns are in book form. Volume I is out of print. Volumes II - IV are $16.50 each, plus tax, indexed, 100 pp. Books are available from the columnist or from McDowell Publications, R 4, Box 314, Utica, KY 42348. Many libraries have these volumes, including the Hawesville Library, Ft. Wayne-Allen County (IN) Library, Rowan County (NC) Library, and the New York Public Library. Original copies are at the Archives, Old Courthouse, Hawesville, KY. (10) Columnist advertises any book she feels will be a help to researchers reached by her column. She will review any books sent to her at no charge. She also does research.

HENRY COUNTY: See Jefferson Co., IN.

HICKMAN COUNTY: See Henry Co., TN.

Mrs. Lucille Bryars Owings published her last genealogy column in 1977. The column was not compiled or indexed. No other information was available.

JEFFERSON COUNTY: See Jefferson Co., IN.

Louisville's *Herald Post*, which reportedly published KENTUCKY KINFOLKS, is no longer being published. The Louisville Free Public Library, 4th and York Sts., Louisville, KY 40203, may have copies of the column. No other information was available.

KNOX COUNTY

Mrs. Patsy Ann Koerner no longer writes GENEALOGY CORNER for *The Barbourville Mountain Advocate*, POB 198, Barbourville, KY 40906. Columns appeared on Thursdays and were not compiled or indexed. No other information was available.

LAWRENCE COUNTY: See Lewis Co., KY (9) & Wayne Co., WV.

LEWIS COUNTY

(1) ANCESTOR HUNTING by Dr. William M. Talley, 110½ Main St., Vanceburg, KY 41179. e-mail address: CXWT@MUSICA.McGILL.CA. (2) Kentucky counties of Boyd, Carter, Greenup, and Lewis; Ohio counties of Adams, Lawrence, and Scioto. (4) Weekly. (6) Families must have lived in above counties. Send family outline with ample facts so readers can recognize the family. (7) Free. (8) Columns not compiled and indexed. If readers want addresses of persons working on the same family or wish to have Dr. Talley search his files to determine what is available, there is a $5.00 initial fee. (9) EASTERN KENTUCKY REFERENCES by Evelyn Jackson and William Talley, indexed, hardbound, 496 pp., $30.50 postpaid. Kentucky residents add 5% sales tax. Book covers Kentucky counties of Lewis, Boyd, Carter, Fleming, Rowan, Greenup, Lawrence, Montgomery, and Nicholas. Book may be ordered from Evelyn Jackson, POB 1834, Ashland, KY 41101.

METCALFE COUNTY: See Adair Co., KY.

MONTGOMERY COUNTY: See Lewis Co., KY (9).

Harry W. Mills, whose column covered the 18 counties encompassed by the original Montgomery County, died January, 1980. His records are not available. He wrote for the *Mt. Sterling Advocate*, the Stanford *Interior Journal*, and the Owingsville *News-Outlook*. The libraries in those towns may have copies of the columns. No other information was available.

NICHOLAS COUNTY: See Lewis Co., KY (9).

OHIO COUNTY: See Hancock Co., KY.

The questionnaire to William J. and Julia Teresa Shall was returned by the U.S. Postal Service. Their long-running column, WESTERN WATERS, has apparently been discontinued. It appeared bi-weekly from February, 1973 in *The Ohio County Times-News*, POB 226, Hartford, KY 42347. Column did not feature queries. Columns are said to be at the newspaper office and some libraries.

GENEALOGICAL NEWSPAPER COLUMNS OF AGNES ASHBY, compiled by Cook. Columns of an experienced genealogist, now deceased, whose columns appeared in the *Ohio County Times*, 1969-1972. Much on Breckinridge, Daviess, Ohio, and surrounding counties. Cemeteries, family data, vital statistics, wills and deeds. Indexed, 163 pp. The book is out of print but should be available in area libraries.

OLDHAM COUNTY: See Jefferson Co., IN.

OWEN COUNTY: See Jefferson Co., IN.

OWSLEY COUNTY: See Breathitt Co., KY.

PERRY COUNTY: See Breathitt Co., KY.

PIKE COUNTY

(1) GENEALOGY NOTES by Sharon D. Warrix, Rt. 1, Box 633, Shelbiana, KY 41562. Phone (606) 432-4904. (6) Queries printed as space permits. If writer has pictures to be published, include SASE if photos are to be returned.

GENEALOGY NOTES replaces Dorcas Hobbs' column, APPALACHIAN ANCESTORS, which appeared bi-monthly on Fridays, in *Appalachian News-Express*, POB 802, 201 Caroline Ave., Pikeville, KY 41501. The column started in November, 1976. Queries had to pertain to eastern Kentucky or western West Virginia. Columns are available at the Pikeville Public Library, but were not indexed. It is assumed that this information is essentially the same for Sharon D. Warrix's column.

Pike County Society for Historical and Genealogical Research, Inc., has published many volumes of Pike County-related historical papers, including marriage bonds and death records. Write the Society, POB 97, Pikeville, KY 41502 for information on those publications.

ROWAN COUNTY: See Lewis Co., KY (9).

RUSSELL COUNTY: See Adair Co., KY.

SHELBY COUNTY: See Jefferson Co., IN.

TAYLOR COUNTY: See Adair Co., KY.

TRIGG COUNTY: See Henry Co., TN.

TRIMBLE COUNTY: See Jefferson Co., IN.

WOLFE COUNTY: See Breathitt Co., KY.

LOUISIANA

GENERAL: See East Baton Rouge Parish, LA, Plaquemines Parish, LA, & St. Tammany Parish, LA.

Marie Wise did not return her questionnaire. Because it is assumed her column is still in publication, the following information is given from the fifth edition of NGCD:

(1) THE CHALLENGE OF GENEALOGY by Marie Wise, RR 1, Box 1022, Sulphur, LA 70663. (2) The state of Louisiana. (3) Column appears in 25 daily and weekly papers in Louisiana. (4) Weekly. (5) 1977. (6) query must have a Louisiana connection. (7) Free. (8) Columns for 1977-1979 available in bound book form for $10.00.

NORTHERN LOUISIANA

Wanda L. Head's SEARCHING FOR FAMILY ROOTS is no longer being written. It was published bi-weekly or weekly from 1984 - March, 1991, and appeared in Homer's *The Guardian Journal*. An index was planned at one time. Queries concerned northern Louisiana. Wanda L. Head wrote INDEX TO CLAIBORNE PARISH MARRIAGE RECORDS, 1849-1910, $19.50 and INSCRIPTIONS TO CLAIBORNE PARISH CEMETERIES, Vols. I to IV, $16.50 each. She had other works in progress. Contact her at POB 30222, Shreveport, LA 71130-0222.

SOUTHERN LOUISIANA: See Jackson Co., MS.

AVOYELLES PARISH

L'HERITAGE DE L'AVOYELLES by Michael D. Wynne no longer appears in *Avoyelles News-Leader*, nor were columns indexed. However, they should be in the Avoyelles Library. No further information was available.

BEAUREGARD PARISH

There is no genealogy column in De Ridder's *Beauregard News*.

BIENVILLE PARISH: See Lincoln Parish, LA & Natchitoches Parish, LA.

Donna Sutton's weekly column in the *Bienville Democvat* and the *Ringgold Progress* was canceled around 1994, due to lack of space. No other information was available.

CADDO PARISH

+(1) ANCESTOR HUNTING by Wanda Volentine Head, POB 30222, Shreveport, LA 71130-0222. (2) Anywhere, but especially the southern states. (3) Shreveport *Times*, since April, 1991; *Guardian Journal*, until 30 March 1991, when it closed its doors after 99 years of publication. (4) Weekly, on Monday. (5) June, 1988 - March, 1991, in *Guardian Journal*; since April, 1991, in *Times*. (6) No requirements, within reason. (7) Free. (8) Columns will be indexed and published yearly. (9) Columnist has numerous publications on northern Louisiana parishes and also does research for those parishes. (10) Columnist accepts books from any area for review. (11) Member of CGC.

NOTE: The above column is the same one that Mildred Watkins wrote weekly from March, 1963 until her death in early 1988. Claitor Publishing Co., apparently out of business, published the columns from 1963-1968 in a hardbound volume with an index. This volume should be available at libraries in the area and in large genealogical libraries. Columns from January, 1969 are on file at Shreve Memorial Library, Shreveport, LA.

CLAIBORNE PARISH: See Northern LA & Lincoln Parish, LA.

DE SOTA PARISH: See East Baton Rouge Parish, LA (9) & Natchitoches Parish, LA.

EAST BATON ROUGE PARISH

Damon Veach's questionnaire was not returned, but the information given in the fifth edition of NGCD is given here:

(1) LOUISIANA ANCESTORS by Damon Veach, 3800 Howard Ave., New Orleans, LA 70140. (2) Entire state of Louisiana. (3) Since 1977 - *Times-Picayune* (Orleans Parish), New Orleans, LA; since 1978 - *Sunday Advocate Magazine* (East Baton Rouge Parish), Baton Rouge, LA; since 1981 - *News-Star-World* (Ouachita Parish), Monroe, LA. (4) Weekly, on Sunday. (5) See (3). (6) Queries must have Louisiana connection through heritage or residence. Mr. Veach will review publications from any state. (7) Free, any length. (8) Columns are not currently compiled and indexed, but there are plans for book formats. (9) IBERVILLE PARISH RECORDS, Vols. 1 and II, $13.50 each; A HISTORY OF POINTE COUPEE AND ITS FAMILIES, $43.50. Order from Mr. Veach at the address given in (1). Mr Veach is also working on three separate parish histories - St. Martin, Iberville, and DeSoto. (10) When Mr. Veach's column appeared in 1967, in New Iberia's *Daily Iberian*, it was called CAJUNS, CREOLES, PIRATES, AND PLANTERS.

GRANT PARISH: See Natchitoches Parish, LA.

George Avery's column, THE VIEW FROM THE HILL, has not appeared in the *Colfax Chronicle* for many years. No other information was available.

IBERIA PARISH

See East Baton Rouge Parish (10) for information about the genealogy column formerly published in New Iberia.

IBERVILLE PARISH: See East Baton Rouge Parish, IN (9).

JACKSON PARISH: See Lincoln Parish, LA & Natchitoches Parish, LA.

LINCOLN PARISH

WHAT'S YOUR LINE, by C. Coleman Crosby, was terminated in May, 1984. Columns were not indexed, but are available for copying at the *Morning Paper* office, Ruston, LA 71270. The column covered the parishes of Bienville, Claiborne, Jackson, Lincoln, Ouachita, and Union. Also, try local libraries.

NATCHITOCHES PARISH

(1) RELATIVE SEEKING by Mrs. Fern Christianson, 1017 Oma St., Natchitoches, LA 71457. (2) Louisiana parishes of Bienville, De Sota, Grant, Jackson, Natchitoches, Rapides, Red River, Sabine, Vernon, and Winn. (3) Column has moved from *Natchitoches Times* to *The Natchitoches Genealogist*. (4) Weekly, in *Natchitoches Times*; semiannually, in *The Natchitoches Genealogist*. (5) No dates given. (6) Keep queries simple. (7) Free. (8) *Natchitoches Times* is on microfilm at Watson Library, Northwestern State University; *The Natchitoches Genealogist* is in the Natchitoches Genealogy and Historical Association Library.

ORLEANS PARISH: See East Baton Rouge Parish, LA, Lincoln Parish, LA, & St. Tammany Parish, LA.

OUACHITA PARISH: see Lincoln Parish, LA, & listing under East Baton Rouge Parish, LA, for a column published in the Monroe *News-Star-World*.

PLAQUEMINES PARISH:

DELTA PIONEERS by Gladys Stovall Armstrong is no longer published. The weekly column appeared from 1981-1984 in The *Plaquemines Watchman* (Plaquemines Parish), Belle Chasse, LA; *The Hammond Vindicator* (Tangipahoa Parish), Hammond, LA; and *The Magnolia Gazette* (Pike County, MS), Magnolia, MS. The column carried queries about deceased persons from Alabama, Louisiana, and Mississippi. Columns were not indexed but should be available in area libraries. Gladys Stovall Armstrong's publications are out of print, but still available at most major libraries in Louisiana: PLAQUEMINES PARISH MARRIAGES, 1866-1898, extracts from newspapers, 56 pp.; PLAQUEMINES PARISH OBITUARIES, 1865-1898, 91 pp.

RAPIDES PARISH: See Natchitoches Parish, LA.

Winston DeVille, C.G., did not return his questionnaire. The information given about his column in the fifth edition of NGCD is below:

+(1) TITLES AND TALES by Winston DeVille, C.G., *Alexandria Daily Town Talk*, POB 7558, Alexandria, LA 71306. (2) No restrictions. (3) *Alexandria Daily Town Talk*; *Ville Platte Gazette*, Ville Platte, LA 70586; and *Teche News*, St. Martinsville, LA 70582. (4) Weekly. (5) 10 November 1985. (6) No restrictions. (7) Free. (8) LOUISIANA...EN PASSANT was published in *Alexandria Daily*

Town Talk from 1966 to 1970 and is now available in book form, $12.50 postpaid. Order from Smith Books, POB 894, Ville Platte, LA 70586. (9) Send SASE for list of Mr. DeVille's extensive writings. (10) Mr. DeVille is a Fellow of the American Society of Genealogists. (11) Member of CGC. NOTE: Mr. DeVille's column, without queries, appears quarterly in American Genealogy Magazine, POB 1587, Stephenville, TX 76401.

RED RIVER PARISH: See Natchitoches Parish, LA.

SABINE PARISH: See Natchitoches Parish, LA.

Marie Wise's column (see GENERAL, under Louisiana) appears in this parish.

ST. MARTIN PARISH: See East Baton Rouge Parish, LA (9).

ST. TAMMANY PARISH

(1) BACKTRACKING by John T. Hunley, POB 613, Madisonville, LA 70447. Fax: 504-626-9361. (2) St. Tammany Parish or Greater New Orleans area connection. (3) Slidell *Daily Sentry-News*, February, 1990-1995, covering research in Louisiana and Mississippi; Covington *St. Tammany News Banner*, February, 1990-1995, covering research in Louisiana and Mississippi; from 1 October 1995 in *St. Tammany News Banner*, covering research areas listed in (2). (4) Monthly, to coincide with St. Tammany Genealogical Society meetings. Earlier columns mentioned in (3) were published weekly. (5) 1 October 1995. (7) Free. (8) *Daily Sentry-News* columns are at the newspaper, POB 910, Slidell, LA 70458. *St. Tammany News Banner* columns are at the newspaper, POB 90, Covington, LA 70434. (10) Publications/books sent for review will be donated to the Louisiana Genealogy Room, St. Tammany Library, Covington, LA.

TANGIPAHOA PARISH: See Plaquemines Parish, LA.

There are currently no columns being published in this parish. Columns that have appeared in the past include the one listed under Plaquemines Parish, LA, and published in *The Hammond Vindicator*. Other columns have appeared, for varying lengths of time, in Hammond's *Morning Sun*, the *Kentwood News*, and Amite's *Tangi Talk*. These papers may be in local libraries. No other information was available.

UNION PARISH: See Lincoln Parish, LA.

VERNON PARISH: See Natchitoches Parish, LA.

WINN PARISH: See Natchitoches Parish, LA.

MAINE

GENERAL: See Cumberland Co., ME & Penobscot Co., ME.

(1) YOUR SIDE OF THE FAMILY by Lauralee Clayton, 19 Trim St., Camden, ME 04843. (2) Column for those with Maine and New Brunswick, Canada, roots and links. (3) *The Courier-Gazette*, POB 249, Rockland, ME 04841. (4) Weekly, on first and third Tuesdays. (5) 1980. (6) For those wishing to know the date a query will appear, send long SASE. For those wishing a copy of the issue with that query, send $1.00 to Circulation, *The Courier-Gazette*, Park St., Rockland, ME 04851. (7) Free. (8) Back columns in scrapbooks and on microfilm, State Archives, Augusta, ME. Not indexed. (10) This column has won three awards as Best Personal Column in the Maine state communications contest, sponsored by the National Federation of Press Women.

Margo Cobb's GENEALOGY appeared bi-monthly in *Maine Life*, and printed queries about Maine ancestry only. Answers printed were from readers, not necessarily the columnist. Maine libraries should have copies of *Maine Life*. No other information was available.

ANDROSCOGGIN COUNTY

The questionnaire to JoAnne E. Lapointe, 985 Turner Street, Auburn, ME 04210, was returned by the U.S. Postal Service, "Forwarding Order Expired." JoAnne E. Lapointe's weekly (on Sunday) column, FRANCO FILE, started about 1986 and covered research in Canada and New England. Columnist did not give the name of the newspaper in which her column appeared, but stated that copies of the paper were on file with the local library [Auburn?]. Columnist was a State Representative and did not have time to do research, but did print items asking for further information. The ending date for the column is not known.

CUMBERLAND COUNTY

(1) WHAT'S IN A NAME? by Erlene Huntress Davis, *Maine Sunday Telegram*, POB 1460, Portland, ME 04104. (2) Maine, New Hampshire, and Massachusetts. (3) *Maine Sunday Telegram*. (4) Weekly, on Sunday. (5) 1952. (6) Please *print* all *names* and *places* in queries. Inquirers must include their names and addresses as answers are sent directly to them. Include at least one date and place, if possible. (7) Queries are free, but please enclose SASE for any replies requested. (8) An index for the 1984 column is $3.00. It is in some county libraries. (10) Please be patient. There is a backlog. Queries are printed in order received. Columnist will search 10 years of columns and send copy of all queries of any surname. Please send $2.00 per surname for this service.

HANCOCK COUNTY: See Penobscot Co., ME (9).

A questionnaire sent to LEGACIES by Danial Smith, % POB 5254, Ellsworth, ME 04605-5524, was returned by the U.S. Postal Service, "Forwarding Time Expired." No other information was available.

KENNEBEC COUNTY

(1) BRANCHES & ROOTS by Thelma Eye Brooks, Central Maine Newspapers, 25 Silver St., Waterville, ME 04901. (2) Kennebec, Lincoln, Penobscot, Somerset, and Waldo counties. (3) *Morning Sentinel* and *Kennebec Journal*. (4) Every other week in New Sunday Edition of both newspapers. (5) *Morning Sentinel*, 15 April 1987; *Kennebec Journal*, May, 1995. (6) At least one Maine connection and one date; prefer one query per each half of an 8½" x 11" sheet of paper. (7) Free. (8) Columns not compiled and indexed for reader reference.

LINCOLN COUNTY: See Kennebec Co., ME.

PENOBSCOT COUNTY: See Kennebec Co., ME.

(1) FAMILY TIES by Connee Jellison, POB 58, Salisbury Cove, ME 04672. (2) Maine, New England, Maritime Canadian Provinces. (3) *Bangor Daily News*. (4) Once a month; queries only. (5) 1976 - 1986; dropped in 1990. In 1991, column was reinstated due to reader response and is still going strong! (6) One name and one date; plus name and address of correspondent. (7) Free. (8) Columnist has all columns in a press book. Copies are also kept at Ellsworth Public Library and University of Maine at Presque Isle. (9) HANCOCK COUNTY -- A ROCKBOUND PARADISE, published by Donning Co., Norfolk, VA, to benefit Grand Auditorium of Ellsworth ME (theater and arts center), over 400 photos (16 in color), indexed, 216 pp., $13.75. Book contains some genealogy, first settlers of over 50 towns, features old homes. (10) Columnist has been an active member of NSDAR since 1975, is a member of Maine Genealogical Society, the president of Amherst Historical Society, and a life member of Maine Old Cemetery Association.

SOMERSET COUNTY: See Kennebec Co., ME.

Virginia T. Merrill wrote SKOWHEGAN FAMILIES from April, 1984, for The *Skowhegan Voice*. Both the monthly column and the newspaper are gone, due to the economy. The final date of publication was not given. Columns had been compiled and indexed and were accessible by mail for a small fee by writing to the columnist at POB 316, Solon, ME 04979. No information was available as to whether Virginia T. Merrill still offers this service. The columnist's articles also appeared occasionally in *Hermon News* and *The News-Maine History*. Those articles contained items on families with Hermon roots, and items of general genealogical interest. Virginia Merrill's column, KNOW YOUR ANCESTORS, appeared in the *Somerset Reporter* from 25 August 1977 to 17 November 1983.

She also wrote a column, OUR ANCESTORS, for *The Cracker Barrel*, from 8 October 1980 to 21 January 1981. She had a complete copy of these sets, with an index, which had not been published. The columnist may still be willing to check these indexes for a fee and SASE. Published 1990: Volume I of MERRILL IN AMERICA, THE FIRST 4 GENERATIONS, DESCENDANTS OF NATHANIEL MERRILL; Volume II was scheduled for publication in 1991 (generations 5 and 6).

WALDO COUNTY: See Kennebec Co., ME.

WASHINGTON COUNTY

(1) DOWNEAST ANCESTORS by Lee Jeffries, 5C Apple Orchard Lane, Calais, ME 04619. (2) Washington County; Campobello; Western New Brunswick, Canada; and Deer Island, Canada. (3) *The Quoddy Tides*, POB 213, Eastport, ME 04631. (4) Monthly. (5) 11 January 1991. (6) All queries should be sent on 3" x 5" cards, with all names typed or printed. Include, if possible, one date and location. (7) Free. (8) Columnist has indexed file. (11) Member of CGC.

MARYLAND

GENERAL: See Williamsburg, VA.

ALLEGANY COUNTY

(1) "OLD PIKE" TRAVELERS, POB 3103, LaVale, MD 21504-3103. (2) Allegany and Garrett counties, MD; Hampshire and Mineral counties, WV. (3) *The Cumberland Sunday Times*. (4) Monthly. (5) 18 December 1983. (6) 50 word limit on queries. No limit to number of queries, but only three from one person per column, on a first-come, first-served basis. Enclose SASE for copy of publication. (7) Free. (8) Back columns are at the paper. (9) RURAL CEMETERIES OF ALLEGANY COUNTY, $27.50 postpaid, 248 pp., hardback.

BALTIMORE CITY

The Baltimore Sun published a series of articles between 1905 and 1908. At one time, the Maryland Historical Society, 201 W. Monument St., Baltimore, MD 21201, would send a list of names covered in the articles (a one page list), upon request. It is not known if this service is still offered. The Society also had a copying service for the articles, if a pertinent name was found.

FREDERICK COUNTY: See Morgan Co., WV.

GARRETT COUNTY: See Allegany Co., MD.

WASHINGTON COUNTY: See Morgan Co., WV.

There is no genealogy column in Hagerstown.

MASSACHUSETTS

GENERAL: See Cumberland Co., ME & Middlesex Co., MA

ESSEX COUNTY

Good Old Days Magazine, which featured a genealogy column, is apparently out of business. No other information was available.

HAMPDEN COUNTY

New England Homestead, which featured a genealogy column, is out of business.

MIDDLESEX COUNTY

The questionnaire to Robert J. Tarte was not returned. His column, TRACE YOUR ROOTS, may still appear each Thursday in the *Middlesex News*, 33 New York Ave., Framingham, MA 01701. It began in 1981 and featured queries relating to all of Massachusetts. Queries could be no more than 35 words, typed or printed, with surnames in capital letters. In the fifth edition of NGCD, it was reported that columns had not yet been compiled and indexed.

SUFFOLK COUNTY

The *Boston Transcript* featured a genealogy column from 1872-1940. The queries and answers columns appeared from 1896. The columns have been indexed. This index and the columns can be found in many larger libraries. The Boston Public Library also has the complete file. At one time, VJR Associates would conduct a search and copying service, but they may be out of business. The address given in earlier editions of NGCD is no longer valid.

MICHIGAN

SOUTHERN MICHIGAN: See Saint Joseph Co., IN.

SOUTHWESTERN MICHIGAN

(1) FAMILY HEIRLOOMS by Carole Kiernan, POB 81, Watervliet, MI 49098. (2) Southwestern Michigan, although there are NO geographical restrictions on queries, as the newspaper is sent to all 50 states. (3) The *Tri-City Record*, "The combined newspaper of the *Watervliet Record, Coloma Courier & Hartford News*," POB 7, Watervliet, MI 49009 -- for subscriptions ONLY. (4) Weekly -- *The Tri-City Record* is a weekly newspaper. (5) October, 1989. (6) Columnist accepts

queries, reunion notices and other information of genealogical interest. Submit information to writer. (7) Free. (8) Compilation and index of the first five years available from the columnist. The newspapers are available at the Watervliet District Library and the Coloma Library. (9) SOUVENIR OF WATERVLIET (Berrien Co), reprint of 1904 original, history, biographical information, 60+ photos, 48 pp., $4.95 + $1.00 postage; RECORDS OF WATERVLIET, BERRIEN COUNTY, MICHIGAN, Volume III, 1846 & 1856 Watervliet Township Tax Records and Watervliet Township First Land Owners compiled by Carole J. Kiernan, 28 pp., $3.95 + $1.00 postage; Volume I, CEMETERY RECORDS; and Volume II, EXTRACTS OF BIRTH, DEATH AND MARRIAGE NEWS, 1890-1894 contact columnist for details. (10) Carol Kiernan is very involved in all of the area's genealogical societies. (11) Member of CGC.

BERRIEN COUNTY: See SOUTHWESTERN MICHIGAN & Van Buren Co., MI.

CASS COUNTY: See Van Buren Co., MI.

GENESSEE COUNTY: See Oakland Co., MI.

HILLSDALE COUNTY: See Williams Co., OH.

LAPEER COUNTY: See Oakland Co., MI.

LENAWEE COUNTY: See Williams Co., OH.

LIVINGSTON COUNTY: See Oakland Co., MI.

MACOMB COUNTY: See Oakland Co., MI.

OAKLAND COUNTY

Virginia Block's HERITAGE HUNT was cancelled. This Sunday column ran from 1981. It appeared first in the *Detroit Free Press* and, after five years, appeared in Pontiac's *Oakland Press*. The column covered research primarily in Genessee, Lapeer, Livingston, Macomb, Oakland and Wayne counties. Contact the columnist about copies of the column. She desires contact with anyone having Oakland County ancestry from any time period. Information on her current columns:

(1) HERITAGE HUNT II and FAMILY ALBUM by Virginia Block, 2911 Olden Oak Lane, #201, Auburn Hills, MI 48321-2149. (2) Ontario, Canada, in addition to the Michigan counties listed above. (Columnist can research queries about early Ontario landowners from her collection and has atlases for 17 counties of Ontario.) (3) FAMILY ALBUM, Pontiac *Auburn Citizens Post* (weekly for the African-American community); HERITAGE HUNT II, *Lake Orion Review, Clarkston News*; and *Oxford Leader*. (4) Weekly. (5) About 1993. (6) Direct question on nature of inquiry with data known, i.e., place born, date of death, time and place of last residence; SASE and cost of photocopying, if needed; prefer 5-generation

pedigree chart. (7) Free. (8) Columns available only in columnist's personal library. (10) Virginia Block also contributes to the *Mature American Monthly*, not a genealogical column per se. She is president of the Pontiac Area Historical and Genealogical Society, which has an extensive collection of Michigan and Canadian material in many other areas for researching early records, books and newspapers.

VAN BUREN COUNTY

(1) GENEALOGY GEMS by Ann Burton, 43779 Valley Rd., Decatur, MI 49045. (2) Berrien, Cass, and Van Buren counties. (3) *Decatur Republican.* (4) Weekly. (5) August, 1987. (6) Query must be 40 words or less. Enclose SASE for copy of column. (7) Free. (8) Columns are on microfilm at the local library. A project is underway to compile and publish the columns. (9) Contact the columnist for a descriptive flyer of her publications. (11) Member of CGC.

WAYNE COUNTY: See Oakland Co., MI.

MINNESOTA

FOLEY COUNTY

At one time, Bonnie M. Trapp was reportedly writing a column called PIONEER PICKINS, for an Oak Park newspaper, but her questionnaire was returned by the U.S. Postal Service. No other information was available.

KANDIYOHI COUNTY

A genealogy column reported in Kandiyohi County turned out to be a column in the quarterly publication of the Kandiyohi County Historical Society and not a newspaper column.

MISSISSIPPI

GENERAL: See Plaquemines Parish, LA, St. Tammany Parish, LA, Forrest Co., MS, Jackson Co., MS, & Winston Co., MS.

Mary Estes Swaney does not write a column called ANCESTRAL TRAILS. No other information was available.

(1) ROOTS 'N RECORDS by Joyce Shannon Bridges, 3413 Fernwood Lane, Shreveport, LA 71108. (2) All counties of Mississippi. (3) *Port Gibson Reveille* (Claiborne County); *Woodville Republican* (Wilkinson County); *Magee Courier* (Simpson County); *Columbia-Progress* (Marion County); and *Simpson County News*. (4) Weekly. (5) 1991. (6) Must have a Mississippi connection. (7) Free. (8) Columnist has back years published and indexed in book form.

NORTHEASTERN MISSISSIPPI: See Winston Co., MS.

NORTHERN MISSISSIPPI: See Lafayette Co., MS.

NORTHWESTERN MISSISSIPPI: See De Soto Co., MS & Tate Co., MS.

SOUTHEASTERN MISSISSIPPI: See Jackson Co., MS.

ATTALA COUNTY: See Jackson Co., MS.

CLAIBORNE COUNTY: See GENERAL, MS.

CLARK COUNTY: See Choctaw Co., AL.

COPIAH COUNTY

Fay Ratcliff's ANCESTOR TRACKING appeared in the *Daily Leader*, Brookhaven, MS 39601, but is no longer published. No other information was available.

DE SOTO COUNTY

Mildred M. Scott's questionnaire was not returned. The following information is given from the fifth edition of NGCD:

(1) UNDER THE FAMILY TREE by Mildred M. Scott, 3067 Laughter Rd. So., Hernando, MS 38632. (2) De Soto County. (3) *De Soto County Times*. (4) Weekly. (5) January, 1982. (6) Connection to De Soto County or northwest Mississippi. No limit on length. Reserve right to edit. Solicit family sketches of early settlers. (7) Free. (8) Columns not compiled. Back issues available at local library and in Chancery Court Clerk's office in courthouse, Hernando, MS 38632. (9) INDEX OF WHITE CITIZENS IN 1870 CENSUS OF DE SOTO COUNTY, $5.00 postpaid; HERNANDO HISTORIC WINDOWS, 1836-1986, $22.00 postpaid. (10) Cemetery survey of county is complete and publication is in process. Write columnist for more recent information about this publication.

FORREST COUNTY

MEET YOUR ANCESTORS, covering Mississippi ancestry, was first written by Dr. Betty Drake, from 1987 in the Hattiesburg *American*, and from 1988 in the Laurel *Leader-Call*. Sandra E. Boyd took over the column in June, 1990 and continued writing it until 10 June 1991, when the new editor decided he did not want to continue featuring a genealogy column. The column is not currently published in either Hattiesburg or Laurel. Back columns are available at McCain Library, University of Southern Mississippi, Hattiesburg, MS 39406-5148.

GEORGE COUNTY: See Jackson Co., MS.

GREENE COUNTY: See Jackson Co., MS.

HANCOCK COUNTY: See Jackson Co., MS.

HARRISON COUNTY: See Jackson Co., MS.

HINDS COUNTY

There are no genealogy columns in the towns of Bolton, Edwards, Raymond, and Utica; letters to those towns were unanswered or returned as undeliverable by the U.S. Postal Service. For a Jackson genealogy column, appearing in the *Clarion Ledger/Jackson Daily News*, see Winston Co., MS.

JACKSON COUNTY

(1) Regina Hines, C.G.R.S., 1222 Highway 90 East, Ocean Springs, MS 39564. In *Mississippi Press*, column is called BRANCHES AND TWIGS; in *Sun Herald*, it is called GENEALOGY.(2) George, Greene, Hancock, Harrison, Jackson, and Stone counties, as well as other southeast Mississippi counties. (3) *Mississippi Press*, Pascagoula, MS, and *Sun Herald*, Biloxi, MS. (4) Weekly. (5) February, 1979. (6) No space limitation, but columnist does edit. A Gulf Coast connection is desirable, but not necessary. Columnist will print queries about lines throughout Mississippi and southern Louisiana and Alabama. (7) Free. (8) Columns are filed and indexed at columnist's office, also at Biloxi, Pascagoula, and Ocean Springs libraries. Columns indexed from 1979-1989. (9) OCEAN SPRINGS, 1892, second edition, historical review of Jackson County in the year it was incorporated, 157 pp., $15.00 postage paid. (10) Copies of former historical column, PAGES OF THE PAST, covering Mississippi counties of Leake, Madison, Attala and Neshoba, available at Carthage (MS) Public Library and Pascagoula (MS) Public Library. Years covered are 1987-1992. (11) Member of CGC.

KEMPER COUNTY: See Bibb Co., AL.

LAFAYETTE COUNTY

(1) ANCESTOR TRACKING by Joan G. Bratton, Route 1 Box 557, Oxford, MS 38655. (2) Northern Mississippi, with Lafayette County queries given first preference. (3) *The Oxford Eagle*, Oxford, MS 38655. (4) Carried irregularly, as time and space permit. (5) May, 1970. (6) Please type or print queries, and present in query form, not as a rambling letter. Be brief, but provide dates, full names, and places of residence. Queries should be on separate sheets, with writer's name and address appearing on each query. (7) Free. (8) Columns are not indexed. When requesting information, please send SASE. (10) The column is sponsored by the Skipwith Historical and Genealogical Society, which also publishes a newsletter with free queries for members. For a list of publications of the Skipwith Society, contact Joan Bratton at the address given in (1). The Society has many Lafayette County Publications.

LAUDERDALE COUNTY: See Choctaw Co., AL.

LEAKE COUNTY: See Jackson Co., MS.

LEE COUNTY: See Pontotoc Co., MS.

LOWNDES COUNTY

At one time, Betty Wood Thomas wrote GENEALOGY AND LOCAL HISTORY for the Columbus *Commercial Dispatch*. The column was published weekly. Back copies are probably at the Lowndes County Department of Archives and History, POB 684, Columbus, MS 39701. No other information was available.

MADISON COUNTY: See Jackson Co., MS.

Laura Boddie Bowers' questionnaire was not returned. The following information was given in the fifth edition of NGCD:

(1) MADISON COUNTY ROOTS: NOTES AND QUERIES by Laura Boddie Bowers, % *Madison County Herald*, 159 E. Center St., Canton, MS 39046. (2) Madison County. (3) *Madison County Herald*. (4) Weekly. (5) About 1988. (6) Prefer requests about Madison County families. Queries may be addressed to the columnist at the newspaper, the library, or her residence, 127 S. Madison St., Canton, MS 39046. (7) Free. (8) Eventually the columns will be included in the library's name index file. Bound volumes of the paper are at the Madison County-Canton Public Library, 102 Priestly St., Canton, MS. (9) The library sells the Madison County history, THE LAND BETWEEN TWO RIVERS, published by Friends of the Library, 1987, 405 pp., $30.00 plus shipping. Contains family histories, illustrated. (10) Many families visit Canton in search of family history. With their permission, the library passes their requests on to the columnist.

MARION COUNTY: See GENERAL, MS & Walthall Co., MS.

NESHOBA COUNTY: See Jackson Co., MS.

NOXUBEE COUNTY: See Winston Co., MS.

PIKE COUNTY: See Plaquemines Parish, LA & Walthall Co., MS.

PONTOTOC COUNTY

CLIMBING YOUR FAMILY TREE by Hazle Boss Neet, C.G.R.S., is no longer published. The weekly column started 29 April, 1982, but no ending date was given. The column appeared in *The Pontotoc Progress* and covered research in Lee, Pontotoc, and Union counties. Columns were never compiled or indexed, but the newspapers are accessible through the local library.

SIMPSON COUNTY: See GENERAL, MS.

STONE COUNTY: See Jackson Co., MS.

TATE COUNTY

Rebecca Haas Smith no longer writes THE FAMILY TIES for the *Tate County Democrat*. The column, which usually appeared weekly, covered research in Tate County and the northwest Mississippi area and began March, 1983. Columns were not compiled and indexed. *Tate Trails*, a genealogical quarterly published by the Tate County Genealogical and Historical Society, POB 974, Senatobia, MS 38668 (80 pp. per year), may still be available. THE FAMILY TIES was written to further interest in genealogy, to get persons with a Tate County connection together with others researching the same families to exchange information, and to aid members of the Tate County Genealogical and Historical Society.

UNION COUNTY: See Pontotoc Co., MS.

WALTHALL COUNTY

Dell Clawson's weekly column, KNOW YOUR ANCESTORS, began in 1977 and was published until about 1980 in the *Tylertown Times*. THROUGH ALL GENERATIONS, a bi-weekly column, appeared in the *Marion County Advertiser* and *Walthall County Advertiser*. Columns related to research in Old Pike County, i.e., Walthall, Pike, and Marion counties. Copies are available at the Tylertown Library. At one time, the columns were available from Dell Clawson for a small fee, but she did not return her questionnaire for this edition of NGCD, which was sent to 4643 Rosalia Dr., New Orleans, LA 70217.

WARREN COUNTY

Although Lamar Roberts, 5560 Gibson Rd., Vicksburg, MS 39180, reportedly writes FAMILY ROOTS, his questionnaire was not returned.

WAYNE COUNTY: See Choctaw Co., AL.

WILKINSON COUNTY: See GENERAL, MS.

WINSTON COUNTY

The questionnaire to Bill Parkes was not returned. The most recent available information about his column is given below:

+(1) FAMILY TREES by Bill Parkes, POB 387, Louisville, MS 39339. (2) All Mississippi counties and anywhere else in America. (3) *Clarion Ledger/Jackson Daily News* (state-wide circulation); *Macon Beacon* (weekly Noxubee County paper); Northeast Mississippi *Daily Journal* (Tupelo), MS. (4) Weekly. Sunday in *Clarion Ledger/Daily News*, and Thursday in *Macon Beacon*. (5) Spring, 1963. (6) No restrictions on queries, but better when brief. No limitations as to area; not just for Mississippi connections. (7) Free. (8) Columns not compiled and indexed. (10) Nancy Randolph Parkes, who originated this column, passed away 20 August 1993. Her husband has continued with FAMILY TREES in her memory. (11) Member of CGC.

MISSOURI

GENERAL: See Holt Co., MO.

NORTHWESTERN MISSOURI: See Page Co., IA.

OZARKS: See Newton Co., MO.

SOUTH CENTRAL MISSOURI: See Howell Co., MO.

SOUTHEASTERN MISSOURI: See Ripley Co., MO.

SOUTHWESTERN MISSOURI: See Laclede Co., MO & McDonald Co., MO.

BUTLER COUNTY: See Ripley Co., MO.

The ownership of Poplar Bluff's *Ozark Beacon* changed, and the new owners did not care to continue Betty Hanks' SHAKIN' THE FAMILY TREE. The Poplar Bluff Public Library, Main and Elm Sts., Poplar Bluff, MO 63901, may have files of the column. No other information was available.

CAMDEN COUNTY: See Morgan Co., MO & Pulaski Co., MO.

CHARITON COUNTY

(1) ANCESTOR SEARCHING by Mae Bartee Couch, Rt. 1, Box 247, Marceline, MO 64658-9634. (2) Primarily Chariton and Linn counties. (3) *Marceline Press* and *Chariton Courier*. (4) Bi-weekly. (5) 13 February 1986. No columns were written between 19 May and 24 November 1988. (6) Query must be typed or clearly written, with surname printed in capital letters. Be concise, but include pertinent information. Columnist will edit queries. Include long SASE, if reply is requested from columnist. Provide as much information as possible for search or query. (7) Queries are free. Write columnist for charges for research. (8) Columns not compiled or indexed. (9) Contact columnist for information on numerous Chariton and Linn county publications, such as cemetery, obituary, census, etc. Columnist is secretary of Genealogy Researchers of Linn County and an active member of the Chariton County Historical Society. The column may carry just queries or just general information or a combination. Columnist works full time researching and compiling. (11) Member of CGC.

CHRISTIAN COUNTY

William A. Yates' THE RIDGE RUNNERS was discontinued in 1982. He did not return the questionnaire, but at one time he could be contacted at POB 237, Ozark, MO 65721, about his current publications and copies of his columns. No other information was available.

DeKALB COUNTY

Jacqueline Combs Rubins did not return her questionnaire, but information from the fifth edition of NGCD is listed here:

(1) Jacqueline Combs Rubins, R.N., POB 226, Cape Canaveral, FL 32920. (2) Primarily DeKalb Co. (3) *DeKalb County Record Herald.* (4) Weekly. (5) October, 1988. (6) None. (7) Free.

(8) DeKalb County Historical Society Library has copies of columns. Columnist has complete copies on floppy disks. (10) Columnist is a member of Missouri Historical Society, and Palm Beach County (FL) and Brevard County (FL) Genealogical societies.

GREENE COUNTY

Lena Wills passed away 19 October 1986. Her column, OZARK GENEALOGY, appeared in the *Springfield News and Leader*, Springfield, MO 65801, and was one of the longest running columns under one name and by one person. It ran from November, 1969. The columns were not compiled and indexed, but copies may be found in New York City Library, Denver Library, Los Angeles Public Library, Dallas Public Library, and others.

HOLT COUNTY

Letha Mowry's WESTWARD HO! was canceled due to lack of queries. Her column appeared from January 1982 in the Mound City *Independent* and covered research in Missouri, Nebraska, Kansas, and Iowa. Columns were not compiled and indexed, but should be available in Holt County libraries.

HOWELL COUNTY

(1) THE FAMILY TREE by Mrs. Irene Kimberlin, 939 Nichols Dr., West Plains, MO 65775. (2) Primarily south central Missouri and north central Arkansas. Locally -- Howell County. (3) *West Plains Daily Quill.* (4) As space permits. (5) 18 November 1982. (6) Queries should be of reasonable length, typed or printed, preferably with the following format: SURNAMES BEING RESEARCHED; submitter's name and address, including Zip code; full name of individuals when possible; include places and dates of events when known. (7) Free. (8) Columns are

accessible at the local genealogical society's library. (9) South-Central Missouri Genealogical Society has numerous publications on Howell County. Send long SASE for a list of publications to 939 Nichols Dr., West Plains, MO 65775. (10) A Howell County and Local History Room and a Newspaper Room have been added to the West Plains Library.

IRON COUNTY

Edna Bond Ripley has discontinued her column, BACKTRACKING, which appeared in the *Mountain Echo* from 25 July 1979. Column was not indexed, but a scrapbook of all the columns is kept by the Saint Louis Genealogical Society. No other information was available.

JACKSON COUNTY

Want Ad Department, *Kansas City Star*, 1729 Grand Ave., Kansas City, MO 64108, accepts paid genealogy advertisements. These appear on Sunday under the Personals classification in the Want Ad section.

LACLEDE COUNTY: See Pulaski Co., MO.

+(1) LACLEDE COUNTY CHRONICLES by Kirk Pearce, 1016 Tower Rd., Lebanon, MO 65536. (2) Southwestern Missouri and anywhere in United States requested. (3) *Lebanon Daily Record*. (4) Bi-weekly. (5) March, 1983. (6) Unlimited queries; will be published as space permits. (7) Free. (8) Columns are not indexed, but are available at local library, and also available at the newspaper office back one year. (9) The Laclede County Historical Society sells: LEBANON CITY CEMETERY BOOK, $13.00; LACLEDE COUNTY CEMETERY BOOK, 3 volumes at $11.00; 3 volumes of MARRIAGE RECORDS OF LACLEDE COUNTY, 1849-1881, $6.00; 1881-1892, $7.50; 1892-1902, $7.50. All of the above books are indexed.

LAFAYETTE COUNTY

The questionnaire to *Lexington News*, POB 279, Lexington, MO 64067, was not returned. The paper may still be printing "Letter to the Editor" type queries at irregular intervals. Columns are at the library. "We primarily publish letters where ancestors are believed to be from this area."

LINCOLN COUNTY

Robert E. Monroe's weekly column, FAMILY TRAILS, is no longer published in the *Troy Free Press and Silex Index*. The column covered Lincoln County primarily, but also Montgomery, Pike, Saint Charles, and Warren counties. Columns were not compiled and indexed for reader reference, but copies of the newspapers should be available in the Lincoln County libraries.

LINN COUNTY: See Chariton Co., MO.

LIVINGSTON COUNTY

There is no newspaper genealogy column published in Chillicothe. The reported column was actually a genealogical publication by E.P. Ellsberry, *The Researcher*, POB 206, Chillicothe, MO 64601.

MARIES COUNTY: See Pulaski Co., MO.

YESTERDAYS, A PAGE FROM THE PAST by Dennis Peterman and Judy Germann, is no longer being written, because of the columnists' busy schedules. The weekly column started March, 1987 and covered research in Maries County and adjoining counties where the Old Maries County families moved. No ending publication date was given. Columns appeared in *Maries County Gazette*, Vienna, MO and *Belle Banner*, Belle, MO. Columns featured queries, family histories, and items reprinted from newspapers of the area, from 1860. Column was instituted to aid researchers and historians with all aspects of Maries County's history and families. Columns were not compiled and indexed for reader reference, but the newspapers are available at the newspaper office and at local libraries.

McDONALD COUNTY

The questionnaire to Bonnie Martin was not returned. Information from the fifth edition of NGCD is given below:

(1) FAMILY LIMB LINES, Genealogy Trees by Bonnie Martin, Current Publications, POB 267, Southwest City, MO 64863. (2) Southwest Missouri, northeast Oklahoma, and northwest Arkansas. (3) *Elk River Current* and *The Current* (approximately 5,000 circulation). (4) Weekly, on Tuesday. (5) January, 1989. (6) SASE and copying charge. (7) Free. (8) The columnist has her own surname index, which is also available at several local libraries, including McDonald County Library and the City-County Library at Neosho, MO. (10) Columnist has done research and genealogy for 39 years, taught some classes, been a speaker, been to Salt Lake City Genealogical Library and several other state libraries, and has compiled several newsletters.

MILLER COUNTY: See Morgan Co., MO & Pulaski Co., MO.

MONTGOMERY COUNTY: See Lincoln Co., MO.

MORGAN COUNTY

The questionnaire to Helen Butts, *Hyway 5 Beacon*, POB 1121, Laurie, MO 65038, was not returned. Her weekly column started in July, 1983 and carried queries in letter form, covering research in Morgan, Miller, and Camden counties. Columns were not compiled and indexed. No other information was available.

NEWTON COUNTY

Rocky G. Macy's ROOTBOUND IN THE HILLS is no longer in publication. Mr. Macy moved from the area and gave up the weekly column, which appeared from 22 September 1987 (ending date unknown) in the *Neosho Daily News*, Neosho MO; *The Laker News*, Ketchum, OK; and *Benton County Daily Record*, Bentonville, AR. The column covered research in the Missouri and Arkansas Ozarks, and northeastern Oklahoma. Columns were not indexed, but are available at the Neosho Library.

NODAWAY COUNTY

Jeanean Totten's 102 COUNTRY COUSINS ran in *The Hopkins Journal* from November, 1978 through 1981. The Nodaway County Genealogical Society, POB 214, Maryville, MO 64468, has back issues of the column, and many publications on the county. The Society also has the files of the now-defunct Graham Historical Society, which contain more than 100,000 cards. Send SASE to find the cost of a particular file. Prices range from, "Free with an order," to $10.00 and up, plus postage, and are based on number of pages of information to be copied. Write: Letha Marie Mowry, Files Secretary, Nodaway County Genealogical Society, 417 So. Walnut St., Maryville, MO 64468-2464.

OSAGE COUNTY: See Pulaski Co., MO.

PHELPS COUNTY: See Pulaski Co., MO.

PIKE COUNTY: See Lincoln Co., MO.

PULASKI COUNTY

The questionnaire to Don Vincent was not returned. His current address: 7305 142nd Ave. East #D, Sumner, WA 98390-8210. Information from the fifth edition of NGCD is given below:

(1) SHARING THE PAST by Don Vincent. (2) Pulaski, Osage, Laclede, Wright, Phelps, Camden, Webster, Texas, Maries, and Miller counties. (3) Richland *Mirror*, Mansfield *Mirror*, and Vienna *Gazette*, all three of which are Missouri newspapers. (4) Weekly. (5) 1980. (6) Queries must deal with families from the ten counties listed, and must mention an approximate date. (7) Free. (9) 800 MISSOURI FAMILIES, Vols. I - V, $25.00 each, 200 pp. each; source materials, reports, compilations; name and place index. (10) Mr. Vincent is the editor of *Heritage Quest Magazine*, a speaker, and a lecturer.

RIPLEY COUNTY

Mrs. Thelma S. McManus, C.G.R.S., retired from writing KISSIN' KIN in 1992. Her weekly column covered research in southeast Missouri and northeast Arkansas. It ran from 1976 in *Ozark Graphic*, which ceased publication in May, 1986. Poplar Bluff's *Daily American Republic* (Butler County) picked up the column in August, 1986 and carried it until 1992. The columnist retains a personal file of the columns. Copies may also be on microfilm at the Missouri Historical Society, Columbia, MO. The column contained very brief hints on genealogical research, items of general interest to researchers, queries, and reviews of books submitted for reviews. Send columnist long SASE for latest flyer on her printed publications: 507 Vine St., Doniphan, MO 63935. Mrs. McManus still does research. (11) Member of CGC.

SAINT CHARLES COUNTY: See Lincoln Co., MO.

SAINTE GENEVIEVE COUNTY

Edna Bond Ripley has no column in the Sainte Genevieve *Herald*.

TANEY COUNTY

Branson's *Ozark Mountaineer* reported it has no genealogy column.

TEXAS COUNTY: See Pulaski Co., MO.

WARREN COUNTY: See Lincoln Co., MO.

WEBSTER COUNTY: See Pulaski Co., MO.

WRIGHT COUNTY: See Pulaski Co., MO.

MONTANA

GENERAL: See Spokane Co., WA.

NEBRASKA

GENERAL: See Holt Co., MO & Lincoln Co., NE.

EASTERN NEBRASKA: See Washington Co., NE.

SOUTHEASTERN NEBRASKA: See Page Co., IA.

WESTERN CENTRAL NEBRASKA: See Lincoln Co., NE.

BURT COUNTY: See Woodbury Co., IA.

There is no longer a column named KIN DETECTORS in Lyons, NE, and neither back columns nor index are available. No other information was available.

COLFAX COUNTY

Apparently Richard J. Makousky does not write GENEALOGICAL TIPS AND TALK for the *Howells Journal*, Howells, NE 68641. No other information was available.

DOUGLAS COUNTY

Lesta Westmore's questionnaire was not returned. Information from the fifth edition of NGCD is given here:

(1) FAMILY TRAILS by Lesta Westmore, *Omaha World-Herald*, POB 57157, Lincoln, NE 68505. (2) *World-Herald* readership area. (3) *Omaha World-Herald*, POB 4244, Omaha, NE 68104. (4) Weekly, on Sunday. (5) 1978. (6) FAMILY TRAILS is primarily a "how-to" column. Queries are selected for publication focusing on those that will be helpful to readers in solving research problems. (7) Free. (8) Copies of back issues of the *Omaha World-Herald* are available at W. Dale Clark Library, Omaha, or Nebraska State Historical Society, Lincoln, as well as at other places. Back columns have been indexed, and columnist will check this index if SASE is included. This does not include a copy of the column. (10) Queries are selected and edited for publication. NOTE: Send SASE for detailed information about column, its requirements, and availability of back copies.

LINCOLN COUNTY

(1) HERITAGE LINES by Ruby Roberts Coleman, 1521 Sunset Dr., North Platte, NE 69101-6463. (2) Western central Nebraska. However, since the columnist may be the only one with a regularly-appearing column in Nebraska, she is not too restrictive regarding counties. (3) *The North Platte Telegraph*. (4) Monthly. (5) September, 1983. (6) Queries will be accepted from persons with ancestry or interest in western central Nebraska; must be 60 words or less; must refer to a specific family; must contain approximate dates and places of residence. For reply, include SASE. (7) Free. (8) Columnist has published the first 10 years of the column in book form, HERITAGE LINES, THE FIRST TEN YEARS, $20.00 postpaid from Ruby Roberts Coleman at the address given in (1). (10) The column not only contains genealogical queries, but articles of historical and genealogical interest on western central Nebraska. (11) Member of CGC.

PLATTE COUNTY

Apparently Elaine Vanek does not write PLATTE VALLEY PIONEERS for the *Telegram*, Columbus, NE 68601. No other information was available.

WASHINGTON COUNTY

(1) DIGGING FOR ROOTS by Mary Jo Kubie, 1172 So. 16 St., Blair, NE 68008. (2) Eastern Nebraska and western Iowa. (3) *Enterprise*, Blair, NE; *Pilot-Tribune*, Blair, NE; *Arlington Citizen*, Arlington, NE; *Missouri Valley Times* (if requested), Missouri Valley, IA. (4) Column appears rarely. (5) 4 December 1978. (6) Queries should give as much information about names, dates, and places as possible. (7) Free. (8) Surname index is available. Indexes available at Blair Public Library and Nebraska State Historical Society Library, Lincoln, NE. All newspapers are on microfilm at the local library and Nebraska State Historical Society. (10) When possible, additional research is done, and query is partially answered in paper.

NEW HAMPSHIRE

GENERAL: See Cumberland Co., ME.

NEW JERSEY

OCEAN COUNTY

There are no genealogy columns in the *Beach Haven Times* or the *Tuckerton Beacon*. No other information was available.

NEW MEXICO

SOUTHEASTERN NEW MEXICO: See Ector Co., TX.

CURRY COUNTY: See Lubbock Co., TX.

QUAY COUNTY: See Lubbock Co., TX.

UNION COUNTY: See Lubbock Co., TX.

There is no genealogy column called TRAILING in Tucumcari.

NEW YORK

GENERAL

Yesteryears Magazine is no longer published. In 1975, this quarterly magazine was accepting paid queries, as long as they had a New York connection. Xerox Corporation had all 18 volumes (72 issues) of the magazine and its indexes, which could be bought as either microfilm or photocopies. No other information was available.

CENTRAL AND UPSTATE NEW YORK: See Onondaga Co., NY.

SOUTHERN TIER: See Tioga Co., NY.

BROOME COUNTY: See Tioga Co., NY.

CAYUGA COUNTY: See Wayne Co., NY.

CHATAUQUA COUNTY: See Erie Co., PA.

CHEMUNG COUNTY: See Tioga Co., NY.

DUTCHESS COUNTY

Neither the *Hyde Park Townsman* nor the Pine Plains *Register-Herald* has a genealogy column.

LIVINGSTON COUNTY

There is no genealogy column in Linwood, and Mrs. John Peters, who formerly wrote a column there, is deceased. Her column reportedly appeared in the *Livingston Republican*, Geneseo, NY 15545. Wadsworth Library, Center St., Geneseo, NY 15545 may have copies of the columns. No other information was available.

MONROE COUNTY

Rochester's *Democrat and Chronicle* dropped YOUR NAME QUIZ many years ago. No other information was available.

MONTGOMERY COUNTY

There is no genealogy column in St. Johnsville's *Courier-Standard Enterprise*.

ONONDAGA COUNTY

(1) Harriett Hall, *Stars* Magazine, *Syracuse Herald-American*, POB 4915, Syracuse, NY 13221. (2) Central and upstate (outside NYC) New York. (3) *Syracuse Herald-American*. (4) Bi-weekly. (6) Query must be 30 words or less, with a central or upstate New York connection, and be typed or printed. (7) Free. (8) Columns are not indexed, but have been compiled and are located at the Onondaga County Public Library, Local History and Genealogical Department. (11) Member of CGC.

ORANGE COUNTY

Peter Osborne, III, no longer writes a local history column for Port Jervis' *Tri-State Gazette*. It began in 1980 and ended around 1990, appearing weekly or bi-weekly.

Photographs were included in the column. Columns are accessible to the public at the newspaper and the local library on microfilm.

OSWEGO COUNTY: See Mayville's column under Wayne Co., NY.

TIOGA COUNTY

Tioga County Historical Society's SOUTHERN TIER PIONEERS was dropped about 1989 because of lack of interest. The weekly column ran from 1967 in the Tioga County Courier. It covered Tioga County and adjacent counties: Chemung, Broome, Tompkins, in New York; and Bradford County, Pennsylvania. Columns are filed and available at the Historical Society. The Tioga County Historical Society's Genealogical Committee will answer queries directly, if they are clearly stated in as few words as possible, contain at least one date before 1890 and concern the Southern Tier of New York State. Send SASE (don't use postal cards). Write the Society at 110 Front St., Owego, NY 13827. The Society may also have some Tioga County publications for sale.

TOMPKINS COUNTY: See Tioga Co., NY.

WAYNE COUNTY

For information regarding a weekly local history column, write Donna Stirpe, Editor, *The Wayne County Star*, POB 430, Lyons, NY 14489.

Elizabeth Caster Mayville's questionnaire was not returned. The information from the fifth edition of NGCD is given here:

(1) FAMILY TREE SEARCH by Elizabeth Caster Mayville, 5452 Brown Rd., North Rose, NY 14516. (2) Wayne, Cayuga, and Oswego counties. (3) *Red Creek Herald*; *Cayuga Chief Chronicle*; *Cato Citizen*; and *Fair Haven Register*. (4) Weekly. (5) 1 March 1979. (6) Queries should be typewritten or printed. There is no limit on length or number; columnist will edit. Include SASE if answer is expected. (7) Free. (8) The columnist is compiling a second book of the columns.

NORTH CAROLINA

GENERAL: See Choctaw Co., AL, Hancock Co., KY, & Williamsburg, VA.

NORTH CAROLINA COUNTIES BORDERING VIRGINIA: See Charlotte Co., VA.

WESTERN NORTH CAROLINA: See Buncombe Co., NC.

ALLEGHENY COUNTY: See Ashe Co., NC.

ASHE COUNTY

(1) TAPROOTS by Sandra Lake Lassen, 1499 Lakeside Dr., West Jefferson, NC 28694. (2) Ashe County, primarily, plus parent county, Wilkes, and adjoining counties: Watauga and Allegheny Co., NC; and Grayson Co., VA. Should have some connection to Ashe, however, for queries. (3) *Jefferson Post*, West Jefferson, NC. (4) Twice monthly, usually 2nd and 4th Thursdays. (5) June, 1992. (6) Short; concise; some connection with Ashe County (which is not near Asheville, a common misconception!); include SASE. (7) Free, but include SASE. (8) Columns will be in the Ashe County Public Library's Heritage Room, West Jefferson, NC. (9) Columnist can provide back copies of columns for $.50 each plus SASE. (10) Column includes local and regional history, genealogical "how to's," human interest. About every third column includes queries. Sometimes there is a several month backlog. (11) Member of CGC.

BUNCOMBE COUNTY

(1) FAMILY HISTORY by Joyce J. Parris, 220 Northwest Ave., Swannanoa, NC 28778-2618. (2) Western North Carolina. (3) *Asheville Citizen-Times*. (4) Monthly. (5) July, 1983. (6) Need approximate dates and places for names. (7) Free. (8) In 1994, published first eleven years by subject matter: FAMILY HISTORY OF WESTERN NORTH CAROLINA. (9) The following works all by Joyce Parris: FAMILY HISTORY OF WESTERN NORTH CAROLINA, soft cover, 218 pp., $21.50; JUSTIS, JUSTUS, JUSTICE FOR ALL: A COMPILATION OF EARLY AMERICAN FAMILY RECORDS, over half on these families in western North Carolina, but covers Swedish and English, 1993, soft cover, 223 pp., $23.00; A HISTORY OF BLACK MOUNTAIN, NORTH CAROLINA AND ITS PEOPLE, 1992, hard cover, 416 pp., $23.00 (only a few copies left); TABERNACLE CEMETERY LISTINGS AND HISTORICAL INFORMATION, 1837-1994, one of the oldest cemeteries in western North Carolina, near Black Mountain, North Carolina, 1994, 70 pp., $23.00 (co-compiled with Robert and Joan Goodson). Note: Prices given include postage and handling. (11) Member of CGC.

CATAWBA COUNTY

The paper which published Mary Jane Rodgers' LINKS AND LINES in Newton is no longer in existence. Catawba County Library, 125 No. College Ave., Newton, NC 28658, may have copies of the column. No other information was available.

CRAVEN COUNTY

There is no genealogy column in the *New Bern Mirror*.

CUMBERLAND COUNTY

Lucile Johnson is retired. Her monthly column appeared in the *Fayetteville Observer-Times*, POB 849, Fayetteville, NC 28302, and covered Cumberland and nearby counties. She wrote about historical homes but always gave family histories of the various owners. She was knowledgeable about Cumberland and nearby counties. The columns may be at the local library. Roy Parker Jr.'s BOOKMARK column, which appears in the *Fayetteville Observer-Times* each Sunday, does report on genealogical books of interest.

EDGECOMBE COUNTY: See Wilson Co., NC.

FORSYTH COUNTY: See Stokes Co., NC.

JOHNSTON COUNTY: See Wilson Co., NC.

NASH COUNTY: See Wilson Co., NC.

PASQUOTANK COUNTY

Roy Brooks' BRIDGES TO THE PAST was published weekly in *Forest City This Week* from 1969-1979. Columns are not available to the public, but the Mooneyham Public Library, Forest City, NC 28043, may have back issues of the paper.

STOKES COUNTY

Robert Carroll did not return his questionnaire. Information from the fifth edition of NGCD is given below:

(1) OLD, ODD & OTHER STUFF by Robert Carroll, Rt. 1, Box 108, King, NC 27021. (2) Stokes County, which included Forsyth County prior to 1849; early Surry when it included Stokes County, 1771-1789. (3) *Danbury Reporter*. (4) Weekly. (5) 30 December 1975. (7) Free. (8) Some of the back columns have been kept by the library in Winston-Salem, NC. (10) This is not a formal column. Columnist is not a professional writer, just a retiree who loves local history and genealogy.

SURRY COUNTY: See Stokes Co., NC.

UNION COUNTY

Monroe's *Enquirer-Journal* reports it has no plans to resume carrying a genealogical query column. No other information was available.

WAKE COUNTY

At one time, Sheila Spencer Stover's RELATIVELY SPEAKING appeared in the *Cary News*, POB 243, Cary, NC 27511. No other information was available. Her questionnaire was returned by the Postal Service, "Attempted, Not Known".

WATAUGA COUNTY: See Ashe Co., NC.

WAYNE COUNTY: See Wilson Co., NC.

WILKES COUNTY: See Ashe Co., NC.

WILSON COUNTY

Hugh Buckner Johnston's questionnaire was not returned. Information from the fifth edition of NGCD is given here:

(1) IT'S HISTORY by Hugh Buckner Johnston, RFD 4 Box 160, Wilson, NC 27893. (2) Wilson County and parent counties, Edgecombe, Nash, Johnston, and Wayne. (3) *The Wilson Daily Times*. (4) The column now appears only occasionally. (5) Column began 11 July 1950 and for many years used the byline LOOKING BACKWARD. (6) No queries are printed. (8) Copies of a great deal of Mr. Johnston's photocopied materials, as well as all the items from *The Wilson Daily Times*, are available in the Wilson County Public Library.

NORTH DAKOTA

RICHLAND COUNTY

Janet Kruckenberg reportedly wrote THE GENEALOGY BUG for the North Wahpeton *Daily News*, beginning in 1981, but no other information was available.

OHIO

GENERAL

(1) FIND YOUR ANCESTORS by Joy Wade Moulton, C.G., F.S.G., *The Columbus Dispatch*, 34 So. Third St., Columbus, OH 43215. (2) This is a general interest column on genealogical research. (3) *The Columbus Dispatch*. (4) Weekly, from 1975 to 1982; bi-monthly, in 1982; monthly from 1983 to 1991; bi-monthly from 1991. (5) 1975. (6) Research questions with Ohio connection answered in one column per month. (7) Free. (8) Columns are at the State Library of Ohio (indexed 1975-1985); Western Reserve Historical Society and New England Historic Genealogical Society (to 1981). (9) GENEALOGICAL RESOURCES IN ENGLISH REPOSITORIES, 648 pp., $32.00, sold with SUPPLEMENT (1992) and UPDATE (1994), $4.75, postage and handling $1.00. (10) Circulation of *The Columbus Dispatch* is 425,000. (11) President of CGC, 1989-1992; First Place in

Excellence in Writing Competition, 1994, Local History and Genealogy; Third Place, 1993, General Interest Columns.

ADAMS COUNTY: See Lewis Co., KY & Brown Co., OH..

(1) OUR HERITAGE by The Adams County Genealogical Society, POB 231, West Union, OH 45693. (2) Adams County only. (3) *People's Defender* and *Manchester Signal*. (4) Monthly. (5) 1979. (6) Query must be centered around Adams County people and history. (7) Free to members of The Adams County Genealogical Society. (8) Columns have not been compiled and indexed for reader reference, although the Society's secretary keeps the columns along with the monthly minutes. (9) Send SASE to Society at the address given in (1) for information concerning its numerous publications. Of note is MARRIAGE BOOK, 1797-1830.

ASHTABULA COUNTY: See Erie Co., PA.

BELMONT COUNTY: See Guernsey Co., OH.

BROWN COUNTY

(1) Brown County Genealogical Society, POB 83, Georgetown, OH 45121. (2) Adams, Brown, Clermont, and Highland counties. (3) Georgetown *News Democrat*; Mt. Orab *Brown County Press*; *The Ripley Bee*. (4) Monthly. (5) 1979. (6) Send an ancestral chart giving the name(s) of Brown County ancestors; give information researcher needs on the surname. (7) Free to members; $1.00 to non-members. (8) Columns compiled and indexed and available at the Society's library. (9) Send SASE to the Society for complete listing of Brown County publications on cemeteries; censuses of 1850, 1860 and 1880; marriage records; and church records. NOTE: The Society has discontinued its genealogy column, LINKS AND CLUES, but does publish an article in the three newspapers listed above just after its monthly meeting, which contains queries, along with library acquisitions, and information on the Society.

BUTLER COUNTY

Jim Newton's monthly column ran from 1984 to about 1991, when he retired. His column covered Butler, Clermont, Montgomery, Preble, and Warren counties and appeared in the *Journal-News*, Journal Square, Hamilton, OH 45011. Columns had not been compiled and indexed for reader reference, but should be available in Hamilton libraries.

CLERMONT COUNTY: See Brown Co., OH & Butler Co., OH.

CLINTON COUNTY: See Fayette Co., OH.

COSCHOCTON COUNTY: See Holmes Co., OH.

CRAWFORD COUNTY

Carolyn J. Ratz no longer writes CRAWFORD COUNTY ROOTS. No other information was available.

DEFIANCE COUNTY: See Williams Co., OH.

FAYETTE COUNTY

Sandy Fackler no longer writes THE FAMILY TREE for the *Record Herald*. The weekly column started in 1987 and covered research in Clinton, Fayette, Greene, Highland, Madison, Pickaway, and Ross counties. Columns featured book reviews and notices, queries, news of upcoming events, and lists of new books at the local library. Columns were not compiled and indexed for reader reference, but the newspaper may be available in local libraries. No other information was available.

FULTON COUNTY: See Williams Co., OH.

Mrs. Vashti Seaman died around 1981, and the *Delta Atlas* no longer runs any genealogy columns. The Delta Public Library has all Mrs. Seaman's columns in book form, and they can be photocopied for $.10 a page. There is a $2.00 or $3.00 library fee for any genealogical reference work.

GREENE COUNTY: See Fayette Co., OH.

GUERNSEY COUNTY

Because of health reasons, Eppie Taft (Marllys Victor) gave up her column, OFF THE TOMBSTONE, around 1993, and no one has replaced her. The column appeared two or three times a month and covered research in Belmont, Guernsey, and Noble counties. It ran from 1977 in *The Daily Jeffersonian*, 821 Wheeling, Ave., Cambridge, OH 43725, and from 1966-1975 in *The Daily Record*, Wooster, Ohio. *The Daily Record* columns were indexed and placed in the Wayne County Library, No. Market St., Wooster, OH 44691. Inquiries to the Guernsey County area may be directed to the editor of *The Daily Jeffersonian*, or to the president of the Guernsey County Genealogical Society, 8583 Georgetown Road, Cambridge. This is an active organization and has contacts with surrounding societies in Belmont County and Muskingum County (Zanesville). A compilation of Marllys Victor's columns has been considered.

HANCOCK COUNTY

At one time Findlay's *The Courier* featured a genealogy column called GRASS ROOTS. The Findlay Public Library, 206 Broadway, Findlay, OH 45840, may have back copies of the column. No other information was available.

HARRISON COUNTY

Cadiz' *County Seat Mirror* has neither a query nor a genealogy column.

HENRY COUNTY: See Williams Co., OH.

HIGHLAND COUNTY: See Brown Co., OH & Fayette Co., OH.

HOLMES COUNTY

JoAnne Stallman's THE MISSING SPOKE is no longer being published in the Holmes County Special of *Times-Reporter*, nor is the paper being published. The weekly column began January, 1983 and covered research in Coschocton, Holmes, Tuscarawas, and Wayne counties. Columns were not compiled or indexed. No other information was available.

JEFFERSON COUNTY

TRI-STATE GENEALOGY is reportedly written by Judy Dobyznski for the *Herald-Star*, Steubenville, OH 43952, but her questionnaire was not returned.

LAKE COUNTY

ANCESTRAL EXCHANGE is no longer published in Painesville's *The Telegraph*. The weekly columns were indexed and are available at Morley Library, 184 Phelps St., Painesville, OH 44077.

LAWRENCE COUNTY: See Lewis Co., KY & Wayne Co., WV.

LICKING COUNTY

There is no genealogical column in the *Newark Advocate*.

MADISON COUNTY: See Fayette Co., OH.

MARTON COUNTY

A column in the *Marion Commentator* ran only a short time. Issues of the paper would be available at the Marion Library and at the newspaper itself. No other information was available.

MIAMI COUNTY

The Tipp City newspaper carries no genealogy column.

MONROE COUNTY

A questionnaire to Catharine Fedorchak, 2808 Cumberland Dr., #1A, Valparaiso, TN 46383-2528, was returned by the U.S. Postal Service, "Addressee unknown." Her column, FAMILY RESEARCHING IN MONROE COUNTY had been published weekly in the *Spirit of Democracy* (published continually since 1844), Eastern & Home Aves., Woodsfield, OH 43793. The column began in 1967 and covered Monroe County and early Noble County. It carried no queries, but some of the columns came from information Mrs. Fedorchak found for people looking for Monroe County ancestors. She had all columns and an index to subjects and/or families. Mrs. Fedorchak compiled 17 volumes of Monroe County records, each with an every-name index. All are now out of print. The copyright to her BELMONT COUNTY BEFORE 1830, is now owned by the Belmont County Chapter, Genealogical Society, which may have reprinted the book. (Work done in conjunction with I. Ochsenhein.)

MONTGOMERY COUNTY: See Butler Co., OH.

MUSKINGUM COUNTY: See Guernsey Co., OH.

NOBLE COUNTY: See Guernsey Co., OH & Monroe Co., OH.

PAULDING COUNTY: See Williams Co., OH.

(1) PAULDING COUNTY PEDIGREE by Caroline Wells Longardner, 7292 Road 176, Antwerp, OH 45813. (2) Basically, Paulding County; sometimes northwest Ohio and/or northeast Indiana. (3) *Paulding Progress* and *Antwerp Bee-Argus*. (4) Two or three times per month. (5) February, 1981. (6) Must have Paulding County genealogy connection or solid local history connection. (7) Free. (8) Columns are being indexed and are accessible through the Paulding Carnegie Library, Paulding, OH 45879. (10) Columnist will include any historical items of general interest pertaining directly to Paulding County or the Ottawa or Miami Indians who were from Ohio. Miami-Erie Canal and Wabash-Erie Canal is also of interest. Paulding had an Ottawa Indian Reservation and two active canals at one time about 1800 (Indians) and about 1840 (canals). Material is welcomed on: the Indian Pontiac; the Great Black Swamp; pioneer times; and folklore.

PICKAWAY COUNTY: See Fayette Co., OH.

PREBLE COUNTY: See Butler Co., OH.

RICHLAND COUNTY

Carolyn Chance Ratz no longer writes YOUR OHIO ROOTS, which ran from December, 1982. *Mansfield News Journal* has an index for its paper.

ROSS COUNTY: See Fayette Co., OH.

SCIOTO COUNTY: See Lewis Co., KY.

SENECA COUNTY

Carolyn Chance Ratz no longer writes a column for the *Tiffin Advertiser*, but the Tiffin-Seneca Public Library has copies of the articles.

TUSCARAWAS COUNTY: See Holmes Co., OH.

WARREN COUNTY: See Butler Co., OH.

WASHINGTON COUNTY

(1) FAMLLY TREE by Ernest Thode, Washington County Public Library, 615 Fifth St., Marietta, OH 45759-1973. (2) Washington and surrounding counties. (3) *The Marietta Times*, 700 Channel Lane, Marietta, OH 45750. (4) Every two weeks, on Fridays. (5) 1993. (6) No queries. (8) Columns are available at the local public library. (10) Second prize, General Interest Columns, CGC, 1994. (11) Member of CGC.

WAYNE COUNTY: See Holmes Co., OH.

Eppie Taft's OFF THE TOMBSTONE appeared in Wooster's *The Daily Record* from 1966-1975. For information about columns, see Guernsey County, Ohio.

WILLIAMS COUNTY

Pamela Pattison Lash's ROOTS AND SHOOTS has been canceled. It was sponsored by Williams County Genealogical Society, 420 Oxford Dr., Bryan, OH 43506. Her column appeared monthly, usually the first week, in the *Bryan Times*, and on a space available basis in the *Montpelier Leader Enterprise*, *Edon Earth*, and *West Unity*. It began in June, 1981, and contained information on researching family history, local Society news, queries, and information on current genealogical materials and books for sale, including book reviews. In addition, there was featured a monthly sketch of a Williams County pioneer. The column was concerned primarily with Williams County, with connections in Defiance, Fulton, Henry, and Paulding counties in Ohio; Hillsdale and Lenawee counties in Michigan; and DeKalb and Steuben counties in Indiana. Compiling and indexing the columns was a planned project for the Williams County Genealogical Society. Columns were being kept in the holdings of that Society, Bryan Public Library, Bryan, OH 43506. The Society had several Williams County publications. Send SASE for descriptive brochure.

OKLAHOMA

GENERAL: See Oklahoma Co., OK.

EASTERN OKLAHOMA: See LeFlore Co., OK.

NORTHEAST OKLAHOMA: See McDonald Co., MO & Newton Co., MO.

SOUTHWESTERN OKLAHOMA: See Comanche Co., OK.

BEAVER COUNTY: See Lubbock Co., TX.

BECKMAN COUNTY: See Comanche Co., OK.

CADDO COUNTY: See Comanche Co., OK.

CIMARRON COUNTY: See Lubbock Co., TX.

COMANCHE COUNTY

(1) Aulena Scearce Gibson, POB 148, Lawton, OK 73505. (2) The column is worldwide in scope. Research ideas are discussed concerning any topic or geographic area the columnist chooses. (3) *Lawton Morning Press*, Lawton, OK. (4) Weekly, on Saturday. (5) 1 September 1979. (6) 50 word limit; must have a southwestern Oklahoma connection. (7) Queries are free, if connected to the southwestern OK counties of Comanche, Stephens, Cotton, Tillman, Kiowa, Jefferson, Grady, Caddo, Washita, Beckman, Greer, Harmon, and Jackson. (8) Columns are accessible to the public on microfilm at the library, but have not been indexed to date. (9) Oklahoma Tract Books (original land entries) have now been indexed by surname. Volunteers at Lawton Library will search one pioneer's name and send copy of page on which entry appears for $5.00; or $1.00, if land description is known. Send request to columnist, at the above address. Enclose SASE. (11) Member of CGC.

COTTON COUNTY: See Comanche Co., OK.

GRADY COUNTY: See Comanche Co., OK.

GREER COUNTY: See Comanche Co., OK.

HARMON COUNTY: See Comanche Co., OK.

JACKSON COUNTY: See Comanche Co., OK.

JEFFERSON COUNTY: See Comanche Co., OK.

KIOWA COUNTY: See Comanche Co., OK.

LeFLORE COUNTY

(1) FAMILY FINDER by Poteau Valley Genealogical Society, POB 1031, Poteau, OK 74953. (2) Mainly LeFlore County, but will also include eastern Oklahoma and western Arkansas. (3) *Poteau Daily News and Sun*; *Spiro Graphic*. (4) Weekly. (5) August, 1984. (6) 50 words or less, and should state who, when, where, and what information is needed. Include long SASE if copy of column is required. (7) Free. (8) Columns not compiled and indexed for reader reference. (9) Send long SASE for list of Society's extensive LeFlore publications. The Society has published 22 volumes on cemeteries, marriages, census records, and funeral home records. (10) P.V.G.S. membership is $10.00 per year, January through December. Members receive *The LeFlore County Heritage*, published in January, April, July, and October.

OKLAHOMA COUNTY

Apparently there is no column by Don Rice in the *N.S.M.P. News*, Oklahoma City.

Mary Goddard's WE THE PEOPLE appeared for the last time on 19 January 1991 in the *Daily Oklahoman*, and she passed away on 28 January 1991. The column had appeared weekly, on Saturday, since 5 November, 1975, covering research in all of Oklahoma. Columns were not compiled or indexed for reader reference. Columns since November, 1981 are in a computer data bank of the Oklahoma County library system.

WE THE PEOPLE continued (staff-written) on its established schedule until February, 1992. The *Daily Oklahoman* then hired Sharon Burns, and the column has appeared since that time in every Saturday issue.

(1) WE THE PEOPLE by Sharon Burns, *Daily Oklahoman*, POB 25125, Oklahoma City, OK 73125. (2) All of Oklahoma. (3) *Daily Oklahoman*. (4) Weekly, on Saturday. (5) February, 1992. (6) Queries must be from or about Oklahoma families. (7) Free. (8) Columns have not been compiled and indexed. Those since November, 1981 are in a computer data bank of the Oklahoma County library system. (10) The Oklahoma Historical Society Library Newspaper Archives, 2100 N. Lincoln, Oklahoma City, OK, has microfilmed all newspapers published since the *Cherokee Messenger* in 1844. Some newspaper issues are missing, therefore incomplete. The *Daily Oklahoman* also maintains a microfilm library of its newspapers. (11) Member of CGC.

(1) IN SEARCH OF FAMILY by Sharon Burns, *Daily Oklahoman*, POB 25125, Oklahoma City, OK 73125. (2) Oklahoma City area. (3) *Daily Oklahoman*. (4) Twice monthly, in Community Section, published Monday, Wednesday, or Friday. (5) 3 March 1992. (6) Column deals with individuals who seek help, have found

family members, or who are searching for lost family members. (7) Free. (8) Columns have not been compiled and indexed.

STEPHENS COUNTY: See Comanche Co., OK.

TEXAS COUNTY: See Lubbock Co., TX.

TILLMAN COUNTY: See Comanche Co., OK.

TULSA COUNTY

Wildcat, the Tulsa newspaper that featured Dorothy Tincup Mauldin's WHAT'S YOUR LINE? is no longer being published. Her column ran from September, 1979. She continued a column for a short time in the *Collinsville News*. Her columns printed queries pertaining to Oklahoma Territory or Indian Territory prior to statehood. Columns were not compiled and indexed. Mrs. Mauldin may still continue to write a column on Indian research for *American Family Records*, a quarterly edited by Virginia S. Foster.

Marmie Apsley no longer writes BACKTRACKING IN GREEN COUNTRY for the *Broken Arrow Daily Ledger*. The column only ran a short time. No other information was available.

WASHITA COUNTY: See Comanche Co., OK.

WOODS COUNTY

Merle Jean Klick-Murrow wrote WOODS COUNTY ROOTS from 1983 until her death in 1991, for the Woods County Genealogists. The weekly column appeared in *Alva Review Courier* and *Woods County News*, covering research in Woods County, Oklahoma Territory; and present-day Woods County, OK. Columns are pasted in a notebook at the Alva Public Library, Alva, OK 73717. Woods County Genealogists plans no further column. M. Erskine wrote the column for a while after that, but no longer does so. No other information was available.

OREGON

BEAVERTON COUNTY

Sherrie A. Styx reportedly writes EXAMINING THE PAST, LOOKING FOR ANCESTORS, in Aloha, OR, but a questionnaire sent to her at Bellingham, WA was returned, marked, "Refused."

COOS COUNTY

There are no longer any genealogy columns in Coos County. Billie Webb's column in the *Coos Bay Empire Builder*, Coos Bay, OR 97420, was last published in 1969.

DOUGLAS COUNTY

There is no genealogy column in Tiller.

LINN COUNTY

Mildred Hawkins has written genealogy columns for weekly newspapers and for *Senior News*. These columns covered research areas in the mid-Willamette Valley; Oregon counties of Lane, Linn, Benton, Marion, Polk, Yamhill, and Clackamas. With the demise of Mrs. Hawkins' columns, there apparently are no longer any genealogy columns in Oregon.

MULTNOMAH COUNTY

There is no genealogy column in the *Portland Northwest Sundial/Sentinel*.

PENNSYLVANIA

GENERAL: See Lebanon Co., PA & Williamsburg, VA.

BERKS COUNTY: See Lebanon Co., PA.

BRADFORD COUNTY: See Tioga Co., NY

BUCKS COUNTY

R.T. Williams, who wrote a genealogy column for the *Pennsylvania Traveller Post*, passed away, and the magazine has ceased publication. No other information was available.

CARBON COUNTY

Frankie M.S. Mousseau, the writer of WHO'S WHO IN GENEALOGY? for *The Times News*, 1st and Iron Sts., Lehighton, PA 18235, passed away. No other information was available.

CRAWFORD COUNTY: See Erie County.

DAUPHIN COUNTY: See Lebanon Co., PA.

W.D. Steigerwalt does not write GENEALOGY IS FUN for a newspaper in Hummelstown.

ERIE COUNTY

Keystone Kuzzins is not a newspaper genealogy column but is the quarterly publication of the Erie Society for Genealogical Research. The quarterly (Feb., May, Aug., Nov.), which began in 1972, runs free queries for members (one per year), and covers research in Erie, Crawford, and Warren counties, PA; Ashtabula County, OH; and Chautauqua Co., NY. Past issues are indexed and both the quarterlies and the indexes are at the Erie County Historical Society Library and Reference Room (non-circulating), 417 State St., Erie, PA 16501, with which the Society is affiliated. Society sells: 1853 ERIE CITY DIRECTORY, 39 pp., $4.00; ATLAS OF ERIE CO., PA, 1865, 64 pp., $35.00 (including every-name index); ERIE CO., PA, NATURALIZATIONS, 1825-1906, 200 pp., $22.50; past issues of *Keystone Kuzzins* are $2.00 each. For further details, write E.S.G.R., Kathy Hansen, Editor, POB 1403, Erie, PA 16512-1403.

JUNIATA COUNTY: See Lebanon Co., PA.

LANCASTER COUNTY: See Lebanon Co., PA & Morgan Co., WV.

LEBANON COUNTY

(1) OUR KEYSTONE FAMILIES by Schuyler C. Brossman, POB 43, Rehrersburg, PA 19550. (2) Lebanon, Dauphin, Berks, Lancaster, Schuylkill, York, Northumberland, Juniata, Perry, and Cumberland counties. Columnist will take queries from all of Pennsylvania, although best results would be for the counties listed, as they are in the newspaper's circulation area. (3) *Lebanon News* (Lebanon County) Lebanon, PA; *Press and Journal* (Dauphin County), Middletown, PA. (4) Weekly. (5) 6 October 1966. Column in its 29th year, with 1484 columns published as of 27 March 1995. (6) query must have a Pennsylvania connection and include at least one date; not over 150 words, unless someone submits a feature article (about 2 pages). (7) Free, as space permits. Subscribers' queries are run first. Enclose $1.00 for a copy of the paper containing query. (8) Columns are at Pennsylvania State Library, Harrisburg, PA; Millersville State College, Millersville, PA; Library of Congress has full set and index up to 6 October 1994; Fort Wayne, IN Library has full set of columns photocopied and indexed; South Central Pennsylvania Genealogical Society, % York County Historical Society, York, PA has made an every-name index; all columns up through about 1988 have been microfilmed and are available at the Family History Library in Salt Lake City, UT. (10) Mr. Brossman intends to write his column at least through 1996, to complete 30 years -- longer, if his health permits.

LEHIGH COUNTY

It has been reported that Schuyler C. Brossman's OUR KEYSTONE FAMILIES appears in the *Allentown Morning Call*, but it has *never* appeared in that paper.

MONTGOMERY COUNTY

Dr. Vernon M. Herron, 275 Anderson Rd., King of Prussia, PA 19406-1940, is said to write a genealogy column, but his questionnaire was not returned.

NORTHUMBERLAND COUNTY: See Lebanon Co., PA.

PERRY COUNTY: See Lebanon Co., PA.

SCHUYLKILL COUNTY: See Lebanon Co., PA.

WARREN COUNTY: See Erie Co., PA.

YORK COUNTY: See Lebanon Co., PA.

SOUTH CAROLINA

GENERAL: See Choctaw Co., AL, Hancock Co., KY & Williamsburg, VA.

CHARLESTOWN COUNTY

(1) DID YOU KNOW? by Ruth W. Cupp, *North Charlestown News*, 1928 E. Montague, North Charlestown, SC 29406. (2) Local genealogy and local history. (3) *North Charlestown News*. (4) Weekly. (5) 12 October 1994. (6) Columnist answers all queries, and tries to help with convenient resources, at no cost. (7) Free. (8) Columns are at the newspaper, and the columnist keeps a set in a scrapbook. (11) Member of CGC.

TENNESSEE

GENERAL: See Hancock Co., KY.

WESTERN TENNESSEE

(1) GENIE by Mrs. Reese J. Moses, (901) 772-4292, 2428 Upper Zion Rd., Brownsville, TN 38012-8065. (2) Mainly western Tennessee. (3) *The States Graphic*. (4) Weekly. (5) January, 1991. (6) Include SASE if personal answer is desired. (7) Free. (8) Columns are in a scrapbook at the local library. (7) Cemetery records are being compiled. (11) Member of CGC.

BENTON COUNTY: See Henry Co., TN.

CARROLL COUNTY: See Henry Co., TN.

DAVIDSON COUNTY

Nashville Banner discontinued its Help Desk in February, 1981. No other information was available.

GIBSON COUNTY

Charles D. Fonville's OUR TENNESSEE ANCESTORS appeared in Humboldt's *Courier Chronicle* from December, 1974 through April, 1975. No other information was available.

HAMILTON COUNTY: See Catoosa Co., GA.

HENRY COUNTY

(1) TENNESSEE TRAILINGS by Gwyn B. McNutt and Sherry C. Paschall, POB 310, Paris, TN 38242. (2) Benton, Carroll, Henry, Madison, Obion, Stewart, and Weakley counties, TN; Calloway, Graves, Hickman, and Trigg counties, KY. However, not limited to those counties. (3) *Paris Post Intelligencer*. (4) Weekly, on Friday. (5) 1977; Marty Ball started writing the column in November, 1986; Trudy Hixson began writing the column in October, 1989; current columnists took over in September, 1993. (6) Queries should be brief but contain enough information to aid readers who may recognize a name; not limited to any particular county. (7) Free. (8) Columns are not indexed, but they are available at the W.G. Rhea Library, or *Paris Post Intelligencer*, Paris, TN. (9) Books available on Henry County: WILLS INDEX 1822-1988, 103 pp., $30.00; MARRIAGES 1868-1880, 168 pp., $25.00; MARRIAGES, 1881-1890, 213 pp., $25.00; MARRIAGES 1891-1900, 249 pp., $25.00; MARRIAGES, 1901-1907, 58 pp., $20.00; CENSUS INDEXES: 1820, 21 pp., $20.00; 1830, 20 pp., $20.00; 1880, 52 pp., $25.00; 1900, 62 pp., $25.00; TAX LISTS; 1827, 31 pp., $20.00; 1836, 51 pp., $25.00; 1845, 34 pp., $22.50; 1890, 64 pp. $25.00; OLD 23rd DISTRICT, 100 pp., $22.50; PEN SKETCHES OF HENRY CO., TN (History of Henry County and some families), 89 pp., $25.00. (10) The W.G. Rhea Library has microfilm of courthouse records from 1822-1968, with land deeds from 1819-1993. On the computer as of April, 1995, are over 30,000 names of persons who have family roots and connections with Henry County. A group of volunteers is now in the process of cleaning loose records from 1821 to the present. Family researcher names available through the column and through the courthouse; send SASE with request.

JACKSON COUNTY: See Trousdale Co., TN.

LINCOLN COUNTY

(1) SPANNING THE YEARS by Jane Warren Waller, 238 Point Clear, Conroe, TX 77304-1276. (2) Lincoln County. (3) *Elk Valley Times*, Fayetteville, TN. (4) Weekly. (5) 1974. (6) Query must pertain to Lincoln County and contain at least one date to establish a time period. (7) Free. (8) Some of the columns may possibly

have been indexed by the Lincoln County Genealogical Society. (9) LINCOLN COUNTY, TENNESSEE PIONEERS is published twice a year, with about 100 pages per year, surname index. The publication started around 1970, and subscriptions are $10.00 per volume, with back issues available. LINCOLN COUNTY, TENNESSEE BIBLE RECORDS, 6 volumes at 200 pp. per volume, hard cover, $15.00.

MACON COUNTY: See Trousdale Co., TN.

Lafayette's *Macon County Times* carries no genealogy column.

MADISON COUNTY: See Henry Co., TN.

OBION COUNTY: See Henry Co., TN.

SEVIER COUNTY

Elaine Rawsten Wells' column in the *News Record* was discontinued. No further information was available.

SHELBY COUNTY

The Independent Journal (and Ray Beeman's genealogy column) of Memphis ceased publication after a short run. No further information was available.

SMITH COUNTY: See Trousdale Co., TN.

STEWART COUNTY: See Henry Co., TN.

SUMNER COUNTY: See Trousdale Co., TN.

TROUSDALE COUNTY

Vernon Roddy's GLIMPSES was published weekly from 4 September 1975 to 17 March 1977, in The *Hartsville Vidette*. The column covered the Trousdale County area from 1750 to the present; Jackson, Macon, Smith, Sumner, and Trousdale counties, along with northern Wilson County. Mr. Roddy is said to be active historically and genealogically, but he did not return a questionnaire sent to 204 Andrews Ave., Hartsville, TN 37074. At one time he sold a 100-page paperback for $8.00, THE LOST TOWN OF BLEDSOESBOROUGH, TENNESSEE, dealing mostly with old Smith, old Jackson, and Trousdale counties, and some other counties in the Upper Cumberland section of Tennessee, from early settlement to 1805. Valuable maps were included.

WEAKLEY COUNTY: See Henry Co., TN.

WILSON COUNTY: See Trousdale Co., TN.

TEXAS

GENERAL: See Gregg Co., TX, Guadalupe Co., TX, & Harris Co., TX.

EAST TEXAS: See Panola Co., TX.

SOUTHEASTERN TEXAS: See Harris Co., TX.

SOUTHWESTERN TEXAS: See Uvalde Co., TX.

WEST TEXAS: See Ector Co., TX.

ANDERSON COUNTY: See Lubbock Co., TX.

ANGELINA COUNTY: See Nacogdoches Co., TX.

ARMSTRONG COUNTY: See Lubbock Co., TX.

BASTROP COUNTY

There are no genealogy columns in Smithville or Elgin. The questionnaire to the Smithville *Times* was not returned, and the column in the Elgin *Courier* has been discontinued. No further information was available.

BEE COUNTY

There is no genealogy column in Beeville.

BELL COUNTY

There is no genealogy column in Belton.

BEXAR COUNTY: See Guadalupe Co., TX.

Illness forced Lloyd F. Oliver to discontinue his genealogy column in San Antonio. Copies of this general, weekly column may be in local libraries. No other information was available.

BLANCO COUNTY: See Burnet Co., TX.

BOWIE COUNTY: See Franklin Co., TX.

J.J. Scheffelin's HERITAGE HUNTING is no longer published. The column covered research in Bowie County, Texas and Miller County, Arkansas and appeared every other Sunday in the *Texarkana Gazette*. The column started about 1980, skipped 9 months in 1983, and resumed in January, 1984, until Mr.

Scheffelin was forced to discontinue the column about 1990 due to blindness. No information was given about location and availability of the columns or the newspaper in which they appeared.

BRISCOE COUNTY: See Lubbock Co., TX.

BURNET COUNTY

The questionnaire to Alberteen Rahe was not returned. Information from the fifth edition of NGCD is listed below:

(1) SHIN OAKS FOLKS by Alberteen Rahe, Burnet County Genealogical Society, % Herman Brown Free Library, 100 E. Washington, Burnet, TX 78611. (2) Texas counties of Blanco, Burnet, Lampasas, Llano, San Saba, and Williamson. (3) *Highlander*, Marble Falls, TX. (4) Monthly. (5) 5 December 1985. (6) No requirements for a query, but Society reserves the right to edit. (7) Free. (8) Columns not yet compiled and indexed for reader reference, but copies are in the Burnet County Free Library, Burnet, TX. (9) BURNET COUNTY HISTORY, Vols. I and II, $30.00 each (Vol. II is family histories); BURNET COUNTY CEMETERY RECORDS, $25.00. Checks should be made payable to Herman Brown Free Library.

CALDWELL COUNTY

The Lockhart *Post Register* genealogy column was discontinued. Copies of the column may be in the Clark Library, 217 S. Main St., Lockhart, TX 78644. No other information was available.

CALLAHAN COUNTY: See Taylor Co., TX.

CAMP COUNTY: See Franklin Co., TX, Gregg Co., TX, & Titus Co., TX.

CARSON COUNTY: See Lubbock Co., TX.

CASS COUNTY: See Franklin Co., TX & Gregg Co., TX.

(1) CASS COUNTY COUSINS by Audrey Rankin, % Cass County Genealogical Society, POB 880, Atlanta, TX 75551-0880. (2) Predominantly Cass County, but at times includes origin of Cass County people. (3) *The Atlanta Citizens Journal*, 307 West Main St., Atlanta, TX 75551. (4) As space allows, at least once a month. (5) Column ran from 1974 until 1983, weekly, or as space allowed, then lapsed for a time; resumed on 9 December 1992, and some 50 columns have been published since that time. Reba Byrd, Kathy Peacock, Bernice Smith, and Louise Martin wrote the earlier series of columns. (6) Queries are used when received; no special requirements. (7) Queries are free in this column, but there is a small charge in CCGS Quarterly for non-members. (8) *Atlanta Citizens Journal* is kept in the public library, both in bound volumes and on microfilm, but columns have not yet

been compiled and indexed for reader reference. (9) Send long SASE for listing of publications the Society has for sale, most of which concern Cass County.

CASTRO COUNTY: See Lubbock Co., TX.

CHAMBERS COUNTY: See Harris Co., TX.

CHEROKEE COUNTY: See Lubbock Co., TX.

CHILDRESS COUNTY: See Lubbock Co., TX.

COLLIN COUNTY: See Denton Co., TX.

COLLINGSWORTH COUNTY: See Lubbock Co., TX.

COMAL COUNTY: See Guadalupe Co., TX.

COOK COUNTY: See Denton Co., TX.

CORYELL COUNTY

CORYELL KIN is no longer published in the *Gatesville Messenger*. For several years, it was run in the *Coryell Kin Quarterly*. The newspaper column started around 1980. Queries were free and were required to relate to Coryell County. Contact CORYELL KIN, % Gatesville Public Library, 811 Main, Gatesville, TX 76528 about back copies of the column and of the Quarterly.

COTTLE COUNTY: See Lubbock Co., TX.

DALLAM COUNTY: See Lubbock Co., TX.

DALLAS COUNTY: See Dorothy Graves' column under Ellis Co., TX.

+(1) FAMILY TREE by Lloyd DeWitt Bockstruck, *The Dallas Morning News*, POB 655237, Communications Center, Dallas, TX 75265. (2) No geographical limit. (3) *The Dallas Morning News*. (4) Every Saturday. (5) Anne Hunt wrote the column from its beginning in 1975 until ill health forced her to give it up in the late summer of 1979. She died Thanksgiving, 1979. Margaret Ann Thetford's first column appeared 10 November 1979. Her last column appeared on 30 May 1991. Lloyd DeWitt Bockstruck took over in 1991. (6) Generally, queries are not accepted. (7) Free. (8) Columns are available at Dallas Public Library, 1515 Young St., Dallas, TX 75201. (11) Member of CGC.

The *Irving Daily News* published a few genealogy columns under the name THE WHISTLE STOP, sponsored by the Irving Heritage Society. The *Irving Daily News* is a very small, local paper, and most people in the area refer to the FAMILY TREE column in *The Dallas Morning News*. No other information was available.

FAMILY ALBUM by James P. Cummings is no longer published in the *Mesquite Daily News*. Columns from 1964 through 1978 are bound and indexed and should be in the Mesquite Public Library, 823 N. Ebrite St., Mesquite, TX 75149.

DEAF SMITH COUNTY: See Lubbock Co., TX.

DELTA COUNTY: See Lamar Co., TX.

DENTON COUNTY

Miss Hollace Hervey's HERITAGE HUNTERS no longer appears in the *Denton Record Chronicle*, because of time limitations. The column started 14 October 1979 and appeared monthly, on the second Sunday, at the newspaper's discretion, covering research in Collin, Cook, Denton, Montague, and Wise counties. It was sponsored by Denton County Genealogical Society, POB 23322, TWU Station, Denton, TX 76204. Upon request, Society members will do research in Denton County. Send long SASE for details and for information about Society publications on the county. Columns are in possession of Hollace Hervey, and are in the process of being indexed. The columnist is also including letters that did not get into the column. Write her in care of the Society.

DeWITT COUNTY: See Guadalupe Co., TX.

DONLEY COUNTY: See Lubbock Co., TX.

EASTLAND COUNTY

+(1) PILGRIMS TO PIONEERS by Jeane Pruett, POB 99, Ranger, TX 76470. (2) No restrictions; any state, county, etc. (3) Sunday edition, *Ranger Times*; *Eastland Telegram*; *Cisco Press*; other county papers as space permits. (4) Weekly. (5) 24 January 1988. (6) Queries should include one date and place. So that readers may help, give as much information as possible. Not imperative, but try to keep to 100 words. Columnist reserves the right to edit. SASE required if copy of printed query is desired. (7) Queries and notices printed free. Reviews require complimentary copy of book, magazine, newsletter, etc. (8) Some back copies of columns available in Ruth Terry Denney Library (new historical preservation and genealogical library); others being compiled. (9) Work is currently being done on an update of the cemeteries of the Ranger area of Eastland County. Readers may write to The Heritage Center, Ranger Historical Preservation Society, POB 320, Ranger, TX 76470. If publications not completed, interested persons' names and addresses will be put on mailing list for notification as each publication becomes available. (10) Columnist will accept other sources for publication of column.

ECTOR COUNTY

Shirley Linder Rad's ANCESTRALLY YOURS was published weekly in *The Odessa American* and covered ancestors in West Texas and southeast New Mexico. Columns were bound and indexed. The Ector County Public Library, 622 N. Lee St., Odessa, TX 79760, may have them.

ELLIS COUNTY

The questionnaire to MISSING LINKS was not returned, but information from the fifth edition of NGCD is given here:

(1) MISSING LINKS by Ellis County Genealogical Society, POB 479, Waxahachie, TX 75165.

(2) Ellis County, including cities of Ennis, Palmer, Bristol, Ferris, Rockett, Midlothian, Mountain Peak, Italy, Waxahachie, etc. (3) *Waxahachie Daily Light*; *Ennis Press*; *Ennis Daily News*; *Red Oak Weekly*; *Midlothian Mirror*. (4) Weekly, on Sunday. (5) 1982. (6) Give at least one full name and one complete date. (7) Free. (8) Columns are in the Ellis County Genealogical Society scrapbook. (9) The Society has published 10 volumes of ELLIS COUNTY CEMETERY RECORDS; 2 volumes of ancestor charts of Society members and friends; and ELLIS COUNTY NATURALIZATION RECORDS. Back issues of the quarterly, *Searchers and Researchers*, are available. New publications: 1880 FEDERAL CENSUS, ELLIS COUNTY; MARRIAGE RECORDS, 3 Vols.; DEATH RECORDS, 3 Vols.; 1850 AND 1860 CENSUS. (10) All queries appearing in MISSING LINKS also appear in *Searchers and Researchers*.

Dorothy Graves did not return her questionnaire, but information from the fifth edition of NGCD is given here:

(1) ANCESTOR TRACKS by Dorothy Graves, POB 384, Italy, TX 76651. (2) Texas counties of Ellis, Hill, Navarro, Dallas, and Tarrant. (3) *Ennis Daily News*. The column also appeared for some years in the *Italy Press*, but that paper has gone out of business. (4) Weekly, monthly. (5) September, 1983. (6) Queries must be legible and to the point. (7) Free. (8) Columns have not been compiled and indexed. (10) Columnist will review booklets, books, etc., if review copy is sent.

EL PASO COUNTY

Mary Margaret Davis did not return her questionnaire. Information from the fifth edition of NGCD is listed here:

+(1) ALL IN YOUR FAMILY by Mary Margaret Davis, % *The El Paso Times*, POB 20, El Paso, TX 79999. (2) No limit to research area. (3) *The El Paso Times*. (4) Monthly, on first Sunday. (5) 1977 (6) One query per letter; otherwise, no special requirements. (7) Free. (8) Columns are not compiled and indexed. They are available to the public at the El Paso LDS Branch Library, 3651 Douglas, El Paso, TX 79903. (11) Member of CGC.

ERATH COUNTY

The questionnaire to M. Carl Weitzel was not returned. Information from the fifth edition of NGCD is listed here:

(1) M. Carl Weitzel, *Empire-Tribune*, POB 958, Stephenville, TX 76401. (2) Erath County. (3) *Empire-Tribune*. (4) Weekly. (5) October, 1986. (6) Send a letter. (7) Free. (8) Back columns are compiled and indexed for reader reference.

FANNIN COUNTY: See Lamar Co., TX.

FISHER COUNTY: See Taylor Co., TX.

FLOYD COUNTY: See Lubbock Co., TX.

FRANKLIN COUNTY

The questionnaire to Linda Stansell was not returned. Information from the fifth edition of NGCD is listed here:

(1) DIGGING CYPRESS ROOTS by Linda Stansell, 1409 Battlefield, Rowlett, TX 75088. (2) Texas counties of Bowie, Camp, Cass, Franklin, Morris, Red River, Titus, and Upshur. (3) *Mt. Pleasant Daily Tribune*. (4) Weekly. (5) July, 1980 - July, 1987; resumed in January, 1991. (6) Query must be clear and contain dates and places. Include SASE for copy of column. (7) Free. (8) Columns not compiled and indexed for reader reference. (10) Books reviewed, with donation of copy.

FREESTONE COUNTY: See Leon Co., TX.

Betty Moss Morrow's DEAR TRAILS ran from October, 1990 to 22 March 1995. The weekly column appeared in *Mexia Daily News*; *Fairfield Recorder*; and *Teague Chronicle* and covered research in Freestone, Limestone, and Navarro counties. Columns are in Clayton Library, Houston, TX.

GALVESTON COUNTY

FROM WHENCE WE CAME by Betty Hart, was published in Texas City for about one year, around 1977. Copies of the column may be at Moore Public Library, 1701 9th Ave. N., Texas City, TX 77590.

GONZALES COUNTY: See Guadalupe Co., TX.

GRAY COUNTY: See Lubbock Co., TX.

GREGG COUNTY

Longview News-Journal no longer carries Nancy Ruff's EAST TEXAS HERITAGE. The column appeared weekly, on Sunday, from November, 1984 to Fall, 1992, and covered research in Camp, Cass, Gregg, Harrison, Marion, Panola, Rusk, Shelby, Upshur, and Wood counties, as well as general Texas inquiries. Columns are at local library. Columnist may have compiled and indexed the columns. She also may have some books on Gregg and Harrison counties. Try contacting her at 13 Iris Circle, Longview, TX 75601.

GUADALUPE COUNTY

+(1) FAMILY TREE by Mary C. Bond, 208 N. Roosevelt Ave., Nixon, TX 78140. Telephone: (210) 582-2876. (2) Bexar, Comal, DeWitt, Gonzales, Guadalupe counties; nearly all Texas counties; will accept queries or items from other areas. (3) *Seguin Gazette Enterprise*, Seguin, TX 78155. (4) Weekly, on Wednesday. (5) 1977. (6) Queries should be typed or printed. (7) Free. (8) Columns not compiled or indexed for reader reference. (11) Member of CGC.

HALE COUNTY: See Lubbock Co., TX.

HALL COUNTY: See Lubbock Co., TX.

HANSFIELD COUNTY: See Lubbock Co., TX.

HARDIN COUNTY

Mrs. Dolly Tavares Wimer reportedly writes FOR THOSE WHO QUESTION for Kountze's *Hardin County News-Visitor*. However, her questionnaire was not returned. The address of the paper is POB 159, Kountze, TX 77625.

HARRIS COUNTY

+(1) TRACING ROOTS, % Kevin Ladd, Director, Wallisville Heritage Park, POB 16, Wallisville, TX 77597-0016. (2) Primarily Texas and the southern states, although most areas of the country are covered periodically. (3) *The Liberty Gazette* (Liberty County), Liberty, TX. (4) Weekly. (5) February, 1990. (6) No requirements, but the number of queries columnist can print depends upon the amount of available column space. (7) Free. (8) Copies available at Wallisville Heritage Park Library. (9) CHAMBERS COUNTY, TEXAS IN THE WAR BETWEEN THE STATES, 245 pp., $22.00. (10) The Wallisville Heritage Park Library houses extensive archives on families of Chambers County, Texas and has information on other southeast Texas families.

(1) YOUR FAMILY TREE by Mic Barnette, 1001 West Loop North, Houston, TX 77055. (2) Entire world. (3) *Houston Chronicle*, This Weekend Section; 850,000 circulation; POB 4260, Houston, TX 77210-4260 (4) Weekly, on Saturday. (5) 2

June 1993. (6) Queries not accepted. (8) Columnist has copy of columns; several individuals, societies, and libraries have copies. (10) Column includes society meetings, seminars and news. It also has news concerning any subject of interest to genealogists, as well as book reviews on books pertaining to genealogy. (11) Member of CGC.

Carolyn Pearson's TIES THAT BIND is no longer published by the *Pasadena News-Citizen*. The local library has files of the newspaper in which the column appeared. No other information was available.

There is no genealogy column in Humble.

The Roadrunner has been erroneously reported as a genealogy column, but it is a genealogical quarterly. For subscription information, contact Chapparral Genealogical Society, POB 606, Tomball, TX 77377-0606.

Catherine Cravy Sims' TRACING ROOTS for *The Baytown Sun*, is no longer written.

HARRISON COUNTY: See Gregg Co., TX.

HARTLEY COUNTY: See Lubbock Co., TX.

HASKELL COUNTY: See Taylor Co., TX.

HAYS COUNTY

The column appearing in the San Marcos *Hays County Citizen* was discontinued. Copies may be at the San Marcos Public Library, POB 907, San Marcos, TX 78666. No other information was available.

HEMPHILL COUNTY: See Lubbock Co., TX.

HILL COUNTY: See Dorothy Graves' column under Ellis Co., TX & Sue Swaner Coffelt's defunct column under Hood Co., TX.

HOCKLEY COUNTY: See Lamb Co., TX.

HOOD COUNTY: See defunct column, YOUR AMERICAN ANCESTRY, under Parker Co., TX.

At one time, Vircy Macatee wrote HOOD HERITAGE for the Hood County News, sponsored by The Genealogical Society, POB 309, Granbury, TX 76048. Her questionnaire was not returned, and no other information was available.

Sue Swaner Coffelt no longer writes REMEMBERING, because of time limitations. Her column reportedly appeared in the *Hood County News*, the *Bosque*

County Globe, and the *Whitney Star*, of Hill County. No other information was available.

HOUSTON COUNTY: See Leon Co., TX.

HUTCHINSON COUNTY: See Lubbock Co., TX.

Bee Holmes' GENEALOGY IS FUN no longer appears in the *Borger News-Herald*. No other information was available.

JACK COUNTY

Mrs. Lucille Garner's weekly column, LOOKING BACK, was dropped when the *Jacksboro Gazette* sold. The column featured queries, stories, genealogies, court records, and covered research anywhere. At one time, JACKSON COUNTY HISTORY, 869 pp., + index, was available from Mrs. Garner for $68.00, 220 W. Thompson, Jacksboro, TX 76056.

JOHNSON COUNTY

There is no genealogy column in the *Cleburne Times Review*.

JONES COUNTY: See Taylor Co., TX.

KAUFMAN COUNTY

There is no genealogy column in Kaufman.

KENT COUNTY

FAMILY CORNER is no longer published in the *Jayton Chronicle*, and there are only a few back issues at the Kent County Genealogical Society Library, in the courthouse at Jayton. No other information was given.

KERR COUNTY

The questionnaire to Ed Syers' OFF THE BEATEN TRAIL was returned by the U.S. Postal Service, "Not Deliverable As Addressed -- Unable to Forward." At one time, the weekly column appeared in 24 newspapers in Texas, covering research in the entire state. The column started in 1960 and carried no queries, touching on genealogy only as it affected Texas history and heritage. The columns were said to be available in book form, in Texas libraries.

LAMAR COUNTY

(1) THE FAMILY TREE, % The Lamar County Genealogical Society, 2400 Clarksville St., PJC Box 187, Paris, TX 75460. (2) Lamar County. (3) *The Paris*

News. (4) Weekly, on Sunday. (5) 1990. (6) Lamar County or northeast Texas connection. (7) Free. (8) Columns are at the Society library, but are not indexed. (9) 1870 LAMAR COUNTY, TEXAS FEDERAL CENSUS by Mary Lane, with every-name index, 304 pp., $25.00 + $3.00 p&h; 1860 LAMAR COUNTY, TEXAS FEDERAL CENSUS, with every-name index $15.00 + $3.00 p&h. Order either of these books from Mary Claunch Lane, C.G.R.S., 1830 W. Washington, Paris, TX 75460. Send SASE to the Society for complete list of Red River and Lamar County books for sale. Send SASE to Ron Brothers, 3125 Clarksville St., #127, Paris, TX 75460 for information about THE DEATH AND CEMETERY RECORDS OF LAMAR COUNTY, TX. (10) Pedigree chart for files at the Genealogy Society Library. NOTE: THE FAMILY TREE appeared weekly in *Lamar County Echo* from 1981, but that newspaper is no longer published. The column covered research in Delta, Fannin, Lamar, and Red River counties. Columns should also be available at the Society library.

LAMB COUNTY

The questionnaire to *Lamb County Leader-News* was not returned, but information from the fifth edition of NGCD is given here:

(1) Joella Lovvorn, Editor, *Lamb County Leader-News*, POB 72, Littlefield, TX 79339. (2) Lamb and Hockley counties. (3) Sunday and Wednesday, in the Letters to the Editor column. (4) Queries printed as received. (6) Queries should be as short as possible and written as a letter to the editor, signed at the bottom, with an address. (7) Free. (8) Queries have not been compiled and indexed.

LAMPASAS COUNTY: See Burnet Co., TX.

There is no genealogy column in the *Lampasas Record*, 316 S. Liveoak St., Lampasas, TX 76550.

LEE COUNTY

There is no genealogy column in the *Giddings Times*, 275 N. Main St., Giddings, TX 78942.

LEON COUNTY

Joyce Dashiell Petty did not return her questionnaire. Information from the fifth edition of NGCD is given here:

+(1) FAMILY TRAILS by Joyce Dashiell Petty, Birch Creek Ranch, Marquez, TX 77865. (2) No restrictions. (3) *Jewett Messenger* (Leon County), Jewett, TX; *Fairfield Recorder* (Freestone County), Fairfield, TX; *Mexia Daily News* (Limestone County), Mexia, TX. (4) Weekly. (5) April, 1981. (6) No requirements for a query, but it is best to have a name, place, and approximate date of an event. (7) Free. (8) August, 1982 - August, 1983 were reprinted and indexed in Family

Trails Magazine. (9) Write Mrs. Petty for more information on Family Trails Magazine, which places emphasis on historical and genealogical aspects of Leon, Freestone, Houston, Robertson, and Madison counties during the early Texas/Republic of Texas period. (10) Back issues of Family Trails Magazine, Vols. I and II, are available from Mrs. Petty at $10.00 each.

LIBERTY COUNTY

There apparently is no genealogy column in *The Cleveland Advocate*, POB 1628, Cleveland, TX 77237.

LIMESTONE COUNTY: See Freestone Co., TX & Leon Co., TX.

LIPSCOMB COUNTY: See Lubbock Co., TX.

LLANO COUNTY: See Burnet Co., TX.

LUBBOCK COUNTY

+(1) KIN SEARCHING by Marleta Childs, POB 6825, Lubbock, TX 79493. (2) Texas counties of Dallam, Sherman, Hansfield, Ochiltree, Lipscomb, Hartley, Moore, Hutchinson, Roberts, Hemphill, Oldham, Potter, Carson, Gray, Wheeler, Deaf Smith, Randall, Armstrong, Donley, Collingsworth, Parmer, Castro, Swisher, Briscoe, Hall, Childress, Hale, Floyd, Motley, Cottle, Anderson, and Cherokee; New Mexico counties of Union, Quay, and Curry; Oklahoma counties of Cimarron, Texas, and Beaver; Morton County, Kansas. (3) *Jackson Daily Progress*; *Amarillo Globe-News*. (4) Weekly. (5) August, 1976; since 1987 in Amarillo. (6) No limit on query length. Any type of genealogical information from readers is welcome. Reviews of new publications are also included. (7) Free. (8) Columns not compiled and indexed for reader reference. (11) Member of CGC.

There is no genealogy column in the *Lubbock Sun*, Lubbock, TX 79408.

MADISON COUNTY: See Leon Co., TX.

MARION COUNTY: See Gregg Co., TX.

MIDLAND COUNTY

There is no genealogy column in Midland.

MONTAGUE COUNTY: See Denton Co., TX.

MONTGOMERY COUNTY

Imogene Kinard Kennedy's SHAKIN' THE FAMILY TREE was published in Conroe's *The Daily Courier*. It was discontinued after about one year, and there was no index. Back issues are apparently not available. Copies of the paper may be at the Montgomery County Library, POB 579, Conroe, TX 77301.

MOORE COUNTY: See Lubbock Co., TX.

MORRIS COUNTY: See Franklin Co., TX & Titus Co., TX.

MOTLEY COUNTY: See Lubbock Co., TX.

NACOGDOCHES COUNTY

(1) KISSIN' KUZZINS, 1614 Redbud St., Nacogdoches, TX 75961. (2) Nacogdoches, Angelina, and Rusk counties. (3) *Nacogdoches Daily Sentinel*; *Henderson Daily News*; *Lufkin Daily News*. (4) Weekly. (5) 1970. (6) queries must be legible, pertain to Texas ancestor. (7) Free. (8) Columns are available in various libraries. Two new books are ready. (9) Send $1.00 for postage for free catalog of available titles. (11) Member of CGC.

NAVARRO COUNTY: See Ellis Co., TX & Freestone Co., TX.

OCHILTREE COUNTY: See Lubbock Co., TX.

OLDHAM COUNTY: See Lubbock Co., TX.

PANOLA COUNTY: See Gregg Co., TX.

Leila B. LaGrone's questionnaire was not returned. Information from the fifth edition of NGCD is given here:

(1) KNOW YOUR HERITAGE by Leila B. LaGrone, 512 Stadium St., Carthage, TX 75633. (2) East Texas, principally Panola and surrounding counties. (3) Column began in *Panola Watchman*, but now appears in *Panola Post* (same publisher). (4) Weekly, on Sunday. (5) January, 1975. (6) Not really a query column, but research into area archives as a "teaser" for families to do research. Columnist also gets many requests. (7) No charge unless columnist is asked to do research. (8) Columns have not been compiled or indexed, but columnist may publish a book in the future. (9) Columnist has published eleven books on the area since 1971. Most are sold out. (10) Three of the columnist's books have been official copyrighted genealogies of 80 to 175 pp. One is a large HISTORY OF PANOLA COUNTY, TEXAS, 1819-1978. Others are on various phases of area history. Columnist is currently working on two more genealogies and spearheading a heritage history library in Heritage Hall Museum. KNOW YOUR HERITAGE was named best Texas genealogy column in 1987 by the Texas State Genealogical Society.

PARKER COUNTY

(1) KISSIN' KIN by Evlyn Broumley, *Weatherford Democrat*, 512 Palo Pinto St., Weatherford,. TX 76086. (2) Parker County and surrounding area. (3) *Weatherford Democrat*. (4) Weekly. (5) About 1970. (6) No set requirements for queries, but they should be of local interest. (7) Free. (8) Columns not compiled and indexed. (10) The column also carries notices of meetings, workshops, how-to, and other items of interest to the genealogist and historian. Columnist will review books and materials upon receipt, after which they will be donated to the Weatherford Public Library for use by the public.

YOUR AMERICAN ANCESTRY by James Pylant has been canceled. The weekly column covered Texas research and appeared in Parker County's *Community News*, as well as the following Texas papers: *Eastland Telegram*; *Cisco Press*; *Ranger Times*; *Rising Star*; *Hood County Review*. It began 6 December 1984 in the *Eastland Telegram*. Newspapers should be available through Newspaper Microfilm Collection, Weatherford Public Library, Weatherford, TX 76086, but microfilming may not yet be completed. Queries from readers were compiled and indexed: Datatrace Systems, POB 1587, Stephenville, TX 76401. Mr. Pylant also may still edit a quarterly, *American Genealogy*. At one time Mr. Pylant could be contacted at the Datatrace Systems address about submitting information (free) to GENEALOGIES OF TEXAS FAMILIES, but this may no longer be accurate information.

PARMER COUNTY: See Lubbock Co., TX.

POTTER COUNTY: See KINSEARCHING, under Lubbock Co., TX.

NOTE: Prior to Marleta Childs' column, KINSEARCHING, Mildred Watkins' ANCESTOR HUNTING appeared in the *Amarillo Globe-News*, from September, 1986. Mrs. Watkins died in 1987, and the *Globe-News* began using Marleta Childs' column. Columns may be filed in Genealogy Department, Amarillo Public Library, Amarillo, TX.

RANDALL COUNTY: See Lubbock Co., TX.

RED RIVER COUNTY: See Franklin Co., TX & Lamar Co., TX.

There is no genealogy column in *The Clarksville Times*, POB 1021, Clarksville, TX 75426.

ROBERTS COUNTY: See Lubbock Co., TX.

ROBERTSON COUNTY: See Leon Co., TX.

RUSK COUNTY: See Gregg Co., TX & Nacogdoches Co., TX.

Len Rives reportedly writes FOOTPRINTS for *The Henderson Daily Times*, POB 1503, Henderson, TX 75652-1503, but his questionnaire was not returned.

SAN SABA COUNTY: See Burnet Co., TX.

SHELBY COUNTY: See Gregg Co., TX.

SHERMAN COUNTY: See Lubbock Co., TX.

SMITH COUNTY

Mildred S. Watkins, C.G., wrote ANCESTOR HUNTING for the *Tyler Courier-Times-Telegraph*, POB 2030, Tyler, TX 75710. Her weekly (on Sunday) column covered general research but primarily the southern states. It started in 1982 and ended with her death in 1987. She was not replaced. Columns are on file at Genealogy Department, Tyler Public Library, Tyler, TX.

SWISHER COUNTY: See Lubbock Co., TX.

TARRANT COUNTY: See Ellis Co., TX.

The questionnaire to TEXAS KIN was not returned, but information from the fifth edition of NGCD is given here:

(1) TEXAS KIN by Patricia Jackson and Paul Campbell, POB 1870, Fort Worth, TX 76101. (3) *Fort Worth Star Telegram*. (4) Weekly, on Saturday. (6) Column prints queries, announcements, and book reviews. (10) Columnists are with Genealogy Section of Fort Worth Public Library.

TAYLOR COUNTY

The questionnaire to PATHWAYS TO THE PAST was not returned. Information from the fifth edition of NGCD is given here:

(1) PATHWAYS TO THE PAST, *Abilene Reporter-News*, POB 30, Abilene, TX 79604. (2) Callahan, Fisher, Haskell, Jones, and Taylor counties. (3) *Abilene Reporter-News*, a major West Texas newspaper. (4) Weekly, on Sunday, in the Lifestyle section. (5) April, 1986. (6) Clarity. (7) Free. (8) All names in the column are being indexed. Abilene Public Library has copies of each article. (10) Independent private researcher, not associated with the column: Jean Mansell, 3774 Wilshire, Abilene, TX 79603.

TITUS COUNTY: See Franklin Co., TX.

The questionnaire to Jewel Dixon Johnston was not returned. Information from the fifth edition of NGCD is listed below:

(1) THE GENEALOGY CORNER by Jewel Dixon Johnston, Rt. 4, Box 10, Mt. Pleasant, TX 75455. (2) Newspaper distributed to Camp, Morris, and Titus counties. (3) *Northeast Texas Chronicle*. (4) Weekly. (5) 1986, in *Citizen's Record*; 1987, in *Midweek* (same paper, new name) sold to *Daily Tribune*. (6) query must have a Texas connection and no more than 100 words. (7) Free. (8) There are plans to publish an indexed compilation of the columns. (9) Local genealogical society sells cemetery records of all cemeteries in Titus County, 2 volumes, as well as the 1850 census of Titus County. Columnist has copies of the above. (10) Columnist is the original editor. She will accept genealogy from readers, and will mail copy of column in which query appears only if SASE is enclosed. Will review books only if free copy is sent.

TRAVIS COUNTY

Colonel Ralph E. Pearson's YOUR FAMILY AND MINE ceased with his death around 1990. His monthly column had appeared since 1938 in Austin's *Cedar Post* and covered research in all areas. Colonel Pearson had also published about 1500 family histories. His research may have been microfilmed by the Family History Library in Salt Lake City.

There is no genealogy column in the *Austin Advertiser*.

UPSHUR COUNTY: See Franklin Co., TX & Gregg Co., TX.

UVALDE COUNTY

FAMILY SECRETS is no longer written by Eva Sanderlin, POB 189, Knippa, TX 78870. Her weekly column covered research in Uvalde County and southwest Texas. It appeared from 1979 in the *Uvalde Leader-News*. Columns are accessible to the public at the newspaper office.

VAN ZANDT COUNTY

GENEALOGY COLUMN by Ruth Stout Abbott, Rt. 3, Box 116, Canton, TX 75103. (2) Van Zandt County. (3) *Canton Herald*; *Wills Point Chronicle*; *Edgewood Enterprise*. (4) Twice monthly. (5) 1989. (6) No queries. (8) Columns are compiled and indexed for reader reference.

WALKER COUNTY

There is no genealogy column in Huntsville.

WHEELER COUNTY: See Lubbock Co., TX.

WILLIAMSON COUNTY: See Burnet Co., TX.

WISE COUNTY: See Denton Co., TX.

Catherine Gonzalez reportedly writes WISE ANCESTRY for the *Wise County Messenger*, POB 66, Rhome, TX 76078, but her questionnaire was not returned.

WOOD COUNTY: See Gregg Co., TX.

UTAH

GENERAL

Nicholas R. Murray did not return his questionnaire. Information from the fifth edition of NGCD is given here:

+(1) NICK NACKS by Nicholas R. Murray, 1866 Homestead Farms, Lane #4, Salt Lake City, UT 84119. (2) Entire USA. (3) *Bear Tracks*. (4) Four times per year. (5) February, 1980. (6) Free queries, but society members and subscribers are given preference. (7) Free. (8) 800 different books published: pre-1900 marriage records by county from 16 states (southern and mid-western). SASE for more information. (10) Society does computerized searches of almost 4 million marriage records compiled by the Society.

SALT LAKE COUNTY

Neither the *Church News* nor the *Deseret News* carries a genealogical column.

UTAH COUNTY

International Finders Magazine is defunct.

WASHINGTON COUNTY

Because of illness, Marguerite W. Robinson discontinued her column, which appeared weekly in the *Color Country Spectrum*. The articles were of a general nature and might be found in libraries in the area. No other information was available.

VIRGINIA

GENERAL: See Hancock Co., KY, Charlotte County, VA, & Williamsburg, VA.

CENTRAL VIRGINIA: See Albemarle Co., VA.

NORTHERN VIRGINIA: See Frederick Co., VA.

SOUTHSIDE VIRGINIA: See Charlotte County, VA.

ALBEMARLE COUNTY

Steven G. Meeks' SEARCHING FOR ANCESTORS? is no longer published. The monthly column appeared from 1982 until about 1990 and covered research in central Virginia, i.e., Albemarle and surrounding counties. It appeared in the *Bulletin of Albemarle County*, Crozet, VA. Columns are available in the Albemarle Historical Collection, Jefferson-Madison Regional Library, Charlottesville, VA.

CHARLOTTE COUNTY

HUNTING FOR ANCESTORS by Mrs. Mildred W. Steltzner, was carried in *The Charlotte Gazette* and *The Kenbridge-Victoria Dispatch* (Lunenburg County) for seventeen years, from about 1970 until 1987, when illness forced Mrs. Steltzner to discontinue the column. The weekly column covered research in Lunenburg and Charlotte counties.

(1) CLIMBING THE FAMILY TREE by Joanne L. Nance, % The N.W. Lapin Press, POB 5053, Charlottesville, VA 22905-5053. (2) Base readership of about 20,000 in Southside Virginia counties and North Carolina border counties. (3) *News and Record* (Halifax County); *The Charlotte Gazette* (Charlotte County); *The Kenbridge-Victoria Dispatch* (Lunenburg County); *The Mecklenburg Sun* (Mecklenburg County). (4) Weekly, on Thursday. (5) 14 January 1988, in *The Charlotte Gazette* and *The Kenbridge-Victoria Dispatch*; later in 1988 in the *News and Record*; since 1990 in *The Mecklenburg Sun*. (6) Any Virginia-based query accepted, with preference given to queries with a Southside connection. Send SASE for copy of column in which query appears. (7) Free. (8) Copies available from the columnist in spiral bound book form, completely indexed: Volume I, 1988-1989; Volume II, 1990; Volume III, 1991; Volume IV, 1992; Volume V, 1993; Volume VI, 1994. Send long SASE for price information. (9) CHARLOTTE COUNTY, VIRGINIA 1816-1850 MARRIAGE BONDS AND MINISTERS' RETURNS, 1987, $22.00; CHARLOTTE COUNTY, VIRGINIA 1764-1771 DEED BOOKS 1 & 2, 1990, $18.00. Postage and handling is $2.00 for the first book ordered, and $1.00 for each additional book. Virginia delivery add 4.5% tax. (10) Column alternately features information on Southside Virginia families, abstracts of county records, research tips, genealogical and historical society news, announcements, and books and periodicals for sale.

CLARKE COUNTY: See Frederick Co., VA.

FREDERICK COUNTY: See Morgan Co., WV.

Wilmer L. Kerns' genealogy column appeared in *The West Virginia Advocate*, which ceased publication after the death of the editor in 1992. Mr. Kerns is considering writing a column for another newspaper. He may be contacted at 4715 North 38th Place, Arlington, VA 22207-2914. His monthly column in *The West Virginia Advocate* began publication in 1982. It covered research in northern Virginia and the eastern panhandle of West Virginia: Clarke, Frederick, Shenandoah, and Warren counties in Virginia; Berkeley, Grant, Hampshire, Hardy, Mineral, and Morgan counties in West Virginia. Columns were not indexed, but Handley Library, Winchester, VA and Hampshire County Library, Romney, WV, have all articles on file in archives or genealogy room. (9) HISTORICAL RECORDS OF OLD FREDERICK AND HAMPSHIRE COUNTIES, VIRGINIA (revised 1992), 430 pp., soft cover, $35.00 postpaid; FREDERICK COUNTY, VIRGINIA: SETTLEMENT AND SOME FIRST FAMILIES OF BACK CREEK VALLEY, (1995), 650 pp., hardcover, $48.00 postpaid.

GRAYSON COUNTY: See Ashe Co., NC.

HALIFAX COUNTY: See Charlotte Co., VA.

Kenneth H. Cook's HALIFACTS ceased with his death in October, 1984. The column had appeared in South Boston's *News and Record* since August, 1979. Mr. Cook had maintained an indexed compilation of the columns, but no information has been received about the disposition of that work. See Joanne L. Nance's listing under Charlotte County, Virginia for a replacement column which began publication in May, 1988.

HAMPSHIRE COUNTY: See Frederick Co., VA.

HAMPTON

Virginia H. Rollings reportedly writes a column from 801 Thomas Dr., Hampton, VA 23666, but no other information is available.

LUNENBURG COUNTY: See Charlotte Co., VA.

MECKLENBURG COUNTY: See Charlotte Co., VA.

NEWPORT NEWS

CLIMBING THE FAMILY TREE in the *Daily Press*, Newport News, VA 23607, has been discontinued, but no other information is available.

SHENANDOAH COUNTY: See Frederick Co., VA.

SMYTH COUNTY

William A. Veselik reportedly writes UP A TREE for the *Smyth County News*. However, a questionnaire sent to him at POB 251, Marion, VA 24354 was returned by the U.S. Postal Service, "Not Deliverable As Addressed -- Unable to Forward."

WARREN COUNTY: See Frederick Co., VA.

WILLIAMSBURG

Dorothy Ford Wulfeck resigned 15 June 1976 from her weekly column for *The Virginia Gazette*. The columns covered research in Virginia, Maryland, North and South Carolina, and Pennsylvania. In 1975, the columns had been indexed for 1959 through 1961. The Williamsburg Public Library, Francis and So. England Sts., Williamsburg, VA 23185, might have copies of the column and the index.

WASHINGTON

GENERAL: See Pierce Co., WA & Spokane Co., WA.

BENTON COUNTY: See Spokane Co., WA.

CLARK COUNTY: See Spokane Co., WA.

FRANKLIN COUNTY: See Spokane Co., WA.

KING COUNTY

Lin Nordeen has *never* written a genealogy column in Seattle or anywhere else.

Bob Staunton reportedly writes a column for the *Bellevue Journal American* or for a Kirkland newspaper, but there has been no other information, and his questionnaire was not returned.

PIERCE COUNTY

Janet G. Baccus' ROUTES TO ROOTS appeared in *Pierce County Herald* and *Nisqually Yalley News*, beginning April, 1983 but was dropped in October, 1988. It was published on the 1st and 3rd Tuesdays of each month, and specialized in Pierce and Thurston counties, and Washington State, plus all other areas. Columns are accessible in Puyallup Public Library newspaper files. At one time, columns were available from Janet G. Baccus, 5817 144th St. East, Puyallup, WA 98373, but that may no longer be accurate information.

SPOKANE COUNTY

(1) HERITAGE HUNTING by Donna Potter Phillips, *The Spokesman Review*, 999 W. Riverside Ave., Spokane, WA 99201. (2) Pacific Northwest, Washington, Oregon, Idaho, Montana, and western Canada. (3) *The Spokesman Review*; *The Columbian* (Clark County), POB 180, Vancouver, WA 98666; *The Tri-City Herald* (Benton and Franklin counties), POB 2608, Kennewick, WA 99302. (4) Weekly, on Sunday, in *The Spokesman Review*; weekly, on Thursday, in *The Columbian*; bi-weekly, on Thursday, in *The Tri-City Herald*. (5) 1986, *The Spokesman Review*; 1993, *The Columbian*; 1992, *The Tri-City Herald*. (6) Must pertain to Pacific Northwest ancestor. (7) Free. (8) Columns compiled and available from the columnist; one booklet covering 1986-1991, then annual supplements. Contact columnist at 2204 West Houston, Spokane, WA 99208-4440 (10) "Please send SASE with your query if you'd like copy of column when it appears." (11) Member of CGC.

THURSTON COUNTY: See Pierce Co., WA.

WHITMAN COUNTY

Heidi L. Dowling, R. Rte. 1, Box 123-B, Colfax, WA 99111, reportedly writes a genealogy column, which has not been compiled or indexed for reader reference, but her questionnaire was not returned. No other information was available.

YAKIMA COUNTY

Yakima Eagle, which featured a genealogy column, is no longer being published. Columns may be at the Yakima Valley Regional Library, 102 N. 3rd St., Yakima, WA 98901. No other information was available.

WEST VIRGINIA

GENERAL: See Nicholas Co., VA.

EASTERN PANHANDLE: See Frederick Co., VA.

WESTERN WEST VIRGINIA: See Pike Co., KY.

BERKELEY COUNTY: See Frederick Co., VA & Morgan Co., WV.

CABELL COUNTY: See Wayne Co., WV.

FAYETTE COUNTY: See Raleigh Co., WV.

GRANT COUNTY: See Frederick Co., VA.

HAMPSHIRE COUNTY: See Allegany Co., MD, Frederick Co., VA, & Morgan Co., WV.

HARDY COUNTY: See Frederick Co., VA.

JACKSON COUNTY

The Reverend Shirley Donnelly, who wrote YESTERDAY AND TODAY, is deceased. His column covered research in Raleigh and Jackson counties and ran for at least 20 years. No other information was available.

JEFFERSON COUNTY: See Morgan Co., WV.

MINERAL COUNTY: See Allegany Co., MD & Frederick Co., VA.

MORGAN COUNTY: See Frederick Co., VA.

Frederick T. Newbraugh's questionnaire was not returned. Information from the fifth edition of NGCD is given here:

(1) WARM SPRINGS ECHOES by Frederick T. Newbraugh, Six Rockwell Circle, Berkeley Springs, WV 25411. (2) Berkeley, Hampshire, Jefferson and Morgan counties, in West Virginia; Frederick County, Virginia; Frederick and Washington counties, in Maryland; and all the Pennsylvania counties formed from old Lancaster County. (3) *Morgan Messenger*, Berkeley Springs, WV. (4) Weekly. (5) Column began in 1957, but columnist did not start accepting queries until about 1980. (6) For Morgan County queries, Mr. Newbraugh will print a considerable amount of information on the families, but for those sending queries from outside of Morgan County, limit queries to 50 to 75 words. queries should be ready to hand to the printer - legible and organized. Please keep query separate from other comments. (7) Free. (8) Columns have been compiled, but some are out of print. (10) Those wanting a copy of the printed query and/or Mr. Newbraugh's comments, if he should know anything helpful, should include long SASE. Typed queries are appreciated.

NICHOLAS COUNTY

The questionnaire to *The West Virginia Hillbilly* was not returned. Information from the fifth edition of NGCD is given here:

(1) *The West Virginia Hillbilly*, Richwood, WV 26261. (2) All counties in West Virginia. (3) *The West Virginia Hillbilly*. (4) This is not a column. The paper devotes a page each week to genealogy. (5) 1957. (6) A simple letter. (7) $10.00 for a one-time insertion that includes all the follow-ups, forwarding, and such. (8) Articles have not been compiled and indexed. (9) *The West Virginia Hillbilly* is published each Monday and is $26.00 annually.

PRESTON COUNTY

At one time Janice Cale Sisler wrote a genealogy column for two Preston County newspapers. No other information was available.

RALEIGH COUNTY: See Jackson Co., WV.

The *Gulf Times* is no longer being published. It carried ABBIE'S GENEALOGY ANSWERS by Abbie Bitney, C.G.R.S. The column appeared weekly from July, 1981, but on an irregular basis from August, 1983. It covered research in Raleigh and Fayette counties; a West Virginia connection was required. "How-to" rather than research was emphasized. Columns are in Raleigh County Library, S. Kanawha St., Beckley, WV 25801.

There is no genealogy column in the *Raleigh Register*, PO Drawer R, Beckley, WV 25802. "Not enough interest," reported the paper.

WAYNE COUNTY

Byron T. Morris' OUT OF THE PAST ceased with his death 16 June 1992. The weekly column (starting date not given) appeared in *Wayne County News* and covered research in Boyd and Lawrence counties, in Kentucky; Cabell and Wayne counties in West Virginia; and Lawrence Co., Ohio. Columns were compiled and indexed for reader reference and are available at Cerelo- Kenova Library, Kenova, WV 25530; and Marshall University Library, Huntington, WV 25701.

WYOMING COUNTY

There is no genealogy column in the *Mullens Advocate*.

WISCONSIN

MILWAUKEE COUNTY

Victoria Wilson's genealogy column is no longer published in 14 Post area newspapers. No other information was available.

SAINT CROIX COUNTY

(1) HISTORIC HUDSON by Willis H. Miller, 226 Locust St., Hudson, WI 54016. (2) Hudson, St. Croix Co., WI. (3) *Hudson Star-Observer*. (4) Every two weeks. (5) 1984. (6) This is not a genealogical column, and there are no queries, but letters are answered. (7) Free. (8) Columns are accessible at Star-Observer Publishing Co., POB 147, Hudson, WI 54016. Star-Observer has a partial index. (9) BITS AND PIECES OF HUDSON HISTORY by Willis H. Miller (1994), 28 pp. (8½" X 11"), (no price given); HUDSON TALES RETOLD is a collection of reprinted historical columns from the *Hudson Star-Observer*, by Willis H. Miller. The book

is in its second printing and is $5.95. Both books available from Star-Observer Publishing Co., at the address given in (8).

SHEBOYGAN COUNTY

(1) FADED GENES by Jan Hildebrand, % Sheboygan Press, 632 Center Ave., Sheboygan, WI 53081. (2) Sheboygan County. (3) *Sheboygan Press*. (4) Weekly, on Sunday. (5) 1986. (6) Single question regarding Sheboygan County genealogy or history. (7) Free. (8) Columns are in the newspapers, which are on microfilm at Mead Public Library. They are also indexed at Sheboygan County Research Center, Sheboygan Falls, WI. (9) SHEBOYGAN COUNTY, 150 YEARS OF PROGRESS, 208 pp., $29.95 + tax; HEART OF SHEBOYGAN COUNTY, SHEBOYGAN FALLS, PLYMOUTH, LIMA AND PLYMOUTH TOWNSHIPS (with genealogy section), $49.95 + tax; CHAIRS (Sheboygan County Chair Manufacturers), $10.00 + tax; LEATHER (Sheboygan County Leather Manufacturers) $10.00 + tax.